OVERCOMING SOCIAL ANXIETY AND SHYNESS

A *self-help guide using Cognitive Behavioral Techniques*

GILLIAN BUTLER

BASIC
BOOKS

A Member of the Perseus Books Group
New York

Published by Basic Books,
A Member of the Perseus Books Group
All rights reserved. Printed in Great Britain.
No part of this book may be reproduced in any manner
whatsoever without written permission except in the case of brief
quotations embodied in critical articles and reviews.
For information, address
Basic Books, 387 Park Avenue South,
New York, NY 10016-8810.

Books published by Basic Books are available at special discounts
for bulk purchases in the United States by corporations, institutions,
and other organizations. For more information, please contact
the Special Markets Department at the Perseus Books Group,
2300 Chestnut Street, Suite 200, Philadelphia, PA 19103,
or call (800) 255-1514, or e-mail special.markets@perseusbooks.com.

First published in the UK in 1999 by Constable & Robinson Ltd.

Library of Congress Control Number: 2008921303

ISBB 978-0-465-00545-1

Important Note
This book is not intended as a substitute for medical advice or treatment.
Any person with a condition requiring medical attention should consult
a qualified medical practitioner or suitable therapist.

10 8 7 6 5 4 3 2

Table of contents

Acknowledgements

The ideas in this book have many sources, and my task has been to bring them together in a way that I hope will be useful. If the book achieves its aim then all these sources should be acknowledged, including the personal as well as the professional ones. Conversations about social anxiety with my family, friends, colleagues, students and patients have all contributed to the shape and content of this book, and these conversations have been going on, intermittently of course, since the early 1980s, when I first became interested in this subject. I have enjoyed them, and I have found them stimulating and interesting. More recent influences, however, have been especially important, and I would particularly like to acknowledge the innovative and creative ideas of four colleagues whose work on social anxiety has helped to change the way in which it can now be treated: David Clark, Melanie Fennell, Ann Hackmann and Adrian Wells.

Introduction

Why a cognitive behavioral approach?

Over the past two or three decades, there has been something of a revolution in the field of psychological treatment. Freud and his followers had a major impact on the way in which psychological therapy was conceptualized, and psychoanalysis and psychodynamic psychotherapy dominated the field for the first half of this century. So, long-term treatments were offered which were designed to uncover the childhood roots of personal problems – offered, that is, to those who could afford it. There was some attempt by a few health service practitioners with a public conscience to modify this form of treatment (by, for example, offering short-term treatment or group therapy), but the demand for help was so great that this had little impact. Also, whilst numerous case histories can be found of people who are convinced that psychotherapy did help them, practitioners of this form of therapy showed remarkably little interest in demonstrating that what they were offering their patients was, in fact, helpful.

As a reaction to the exclusivity of psychodynamic therapies and the slender evidence for its usefulness, in the 1950s and 1960s a set of techniques was developed, broadly collectively termed 'behavior therapy'. These techniques shared two basic features. First, they aimed to remove symptoms (such as anxiety) by dealing with those symptoms themselves, rather than their deep-seated underlying historical causes. Second, they were techniques, loosely related to what laboratory psychologists were finding out about the mechanisms of learning, which were formulated in testable terms. Indeed, practitioners of behavior therapy were committed to using techniques of proven value or, at worst, of a form which could potentially be put to the test. The area where these techniques proved of most value was in the treatment of anxiety disorders, especially specific phobias (such as fear of animals or heights) and agoraphobia, both notoriously difficult to treat using conventional psychotherapies.

After an initial flush of enthusiasm, discontent with behavior therapy grew. There were a number of reasons for this, an important one of which was the fact that behavior therapy did not deal with the internal thoughts which were so obviously central to the distress that patients were experiencing. In this context, the fact that behavior therapy proved so inadequate when it came to the treatment of depression highlighted the need for major revision. In the late 1960s and early 1970s a treatment was developed specifically for depression called 'cognitive therapy'. The pioneer in this enterprise was an American psychiatrist, Professor Aaron T. Beck, who developed a theory of depression which emphasized the importance of people's depressed styles of thinking. He also specified a new form of therapy. It would not be an exaggeration to say that Beck's work has changed the nature of psychotherapy, not just for depression but for a range of psychological problems.

In recent years the cognitive techniques introduced by Beck have been merged with the techniques developed earlier by the behavior therapists to produce a body of theory and practice which has come to be known as 'cognitive behavior therapy'. There are two main reasons why this form of treatment has come to be so important within the field of psychotherapy. First, cognitive therapy for depression, as originally described by Beck and developed by his successors, has been subjected to the strictest scientific testing; and it has been found to be a highly successful treatment for a significant proportion of cases of depression. Not only has it proved to be as effective as the best alternative treatments (except in the most severe cases, where medication is required), but some studies suggest that people treated successfully with cognitive behavior therapy are less likely to experience a later recurrence of their depression than people treated successfully with other forms of therapy (such as antidepressant medication). Second, it has become clear that specific patterns of thinking are associated with a range of psychological problems and that treatments which deal with these styles of thinking are highly effective. So, specific cognitive behavioral treatments have been developed for anxiety disorders, like panic disorder, generalized anxiety disorder, specific phobias and social phobia, obsessive compulsive disorders, and hypochondriasis (health anxiety), as well as for other conditions such as compulsive gambling, alcohol and drug addiction, and eating disorders like bulimia nervosa and binge-eating disorder. Indeed, cognitive behavioral techniques have a wide application beyond the narrow categories of psychological disorders: they have been applied effectively, for example, to helping people with low self-esteem and those with marital difficulties.

At any one time almost 10 per cent of the general population is suffering from depression, and more than 10 per cent has one or other of the anxiety disorders. Many others have a range of psychological problems and personal difficulties. It is of the greatest importance that treatments of proven effectiveness are developed. However, even when the armoury of therapies is, as it were, full, there remains a very great problem – namely that the delivery of treatment is expensive and the resources are not going to be available evermore. Whilst this shortfall could be met by lots of people helping themselves, commonly the natural inclination to make oneself feel better in the present is to do precisely those things which perpetuate or even exacerbate one's problems. For example, the person with agoraphobia will stay at home to prevent the possibility of an anxiety attack; and the person with bulimia nervosa will avoid eating all potentially fattening foods. Whilst such strategies might resolve some immediate crisis, they leave the underlying problem intact and provide no real help in dealing with future difficulties.

So, there is a twin problem here: although effective treatments have been developed, they are not widely available;

and when people try to help themselves they often make matters worse. In recent years the community of cognitive behavior therapists have responded to this situation. What they have done is to take the principles and techniques of specific cognitive behavior therapies for particular problems and represent them in self-help manuals. These manuals specify a systematic program of treatment which the individual sufferer is advised to work through to overcome their difficulties. In this way, the cognitive behavioral therapeutic techniques of proven value are being made available on the widest possible basis.

Self-help manuals are never going to replace therapists. Many people will need individual treatment from a qualified therapist. It is also the case that, despite the widespread success of cognitive behavioral therapy, some people will not respond to it and will need one of the other treatments available. Nevertheless, although research on the use of cognitive behavioral self-help manuals is at an early stage, the work done to date indicates that for a very great many people such a manual will prove sufficient for them to overcome their problems without professional help.

Many people suffer silently and secretly for years. Sometimes appropriate help is not forthcoming despite their efforts to find it. Sometimes they feel too ashamed or guilty to reveal their problems to anyone. For many of these people the cognitive behavioral self-help manuals will provide a lifeline to recovery and a better future.

Professor Peter Cooper
The University of Reading

A note of caution

In order to overcome a problem it is important to understand it. Although it may be tempting to skip this section of the book, and to start working on the problem right away, there is much to be gained from reading through the five chapters of Part One. The first one describes the problem of social anxiety, and will help you to find out whether this is indeed the problem you want to read about and work on (or encourage someone else to work on). It helps you to recognize the different forms the problem can take and the different ways in which it can affect you. The second chapter is about shyness, and describes some of the similarities and differences between social anxiety and shyness. In the rest of the book the term *social anxiety* is used to refer to both, as they have similar symptoms, with similar effects, and overcoming them involves using similar strategies.

The third chapter explains the central part played by thinking in social anxiety, and introduces some ideas about what needs to change if the problem is going to improve. The fourth chapter attempts to answer one of the most common questions that people who feel socially anxious ask: where did the problem come from? Finally, the fifth chapter explains how we understand what is going on in social anxiety, enabling us to pinpoint the things that need to be worked on in order to overcome the problem.

PART ONE

Understanding Social Anxiety

1

What is social anxiety

Social anxiety is a shorthand term that describes the fear, nervousness and apprehension most people at times experience in their relationships with other people. Some people who suffer from social anxiety would say they were shy, and may have been shy all their lives, but some people who are not shy also suffer from social anxiety. So shyness is not the whole story. Social anxiety strikes people when they think that they might do something that will be humiliating or embarrassing. Social anxiety makes you think that other people are judging you, and doing so in a negative way, because of something you said or did. Of course, the fear that you will do something humiliating or embarrassing is inhibiting, and it also makes you self-aware: conscious of the possibility that you might indeed do such a thing. Who would want to get into conversation if they thought that doing so would only reveal their clumsiness, or inadequacy, or tendency to blush? Socially anxious people tend to assume that their interactions with others will be painfully revealing: that others will notice their weaknesses or awkwardness; that they will be dismissed, ignored, criticized or rejected for not behaving more acceptably.

Seeing things this way makes it hard to interact naturally with people, and difficult to talk, listen or make friends. Often it leads to isolation and loneliness, and for many people one of the sadnesses of suffering from this problem is that it prevents them becoming intimate with other people, or finding a partner with whom to share their lives.

Socially anxious people usually feel friendly towards others and certainly have their fair share of the positive characteristics that other people appreciate. They may have a sense of fun, be energetic and generous, kind and understanding, serious, amusing, quiet or lively, and they spontaneously behave in these ways when they feel at ease. But feeling at ease in company is so hard for them, and makes them so anxious, that these qualities are often hidden from view. The anxiety interferes with their expression, and the ability to display them may have gone rusty from lack of use. Indeed, socially anxious people may have altogether lost belief in their likeable qualities together with their self-confidence. One of the rewards of learning to overcome social anxiety is that it enables you to express aspects of yourself that may previously have been stifled, and allows you to enjoy, rather than to fear, being yourself. It allows you to discover, or to rediscover, yourself.

Defining the problem

Definitions are useful because they help us to focus on the features of social anxiety that make it problematic – that cause the pain and prolong the agony.

Social anxiety is normal. Everybody feels it sometimes (so everyone knows to some degree what it is like), and it would be absurd for any of us to suppose that we would never feel socially anxious again. For this reason it helps to start by defining when social anxiety becomes a problem, and thinking clearly about what it is that needs to change when it interferes with your life. First, if social anxiety is normal, then it will never go away, whatever you do. So, rather than attempting the impossible, and seeking a 'cure', energy is better spent learning how to reduce its painful aspects and consequences, so that it no longer causes distress and interferes with your life.

The kind of social anxiety, and amount of it, that qualifies someone for a diagnosis using the term *social phobia* is to be found in the *Diagnostic and Statistical Manual of the American Psychiatric Association (DSM-IV, 1994). The manual sets out four main criteria:*

1 *A marked and persistent fear of one or more social or perform-ance situations in which the person is exposed to unfamiliar people or to possible scrutiny by others. The individual fears that he or she will act in a way (or show anxiety symptoms) that will be humiliating or embarrassing.* Note that people with social phobia may not actually *do* anything humil-iating or embarrassing; they only have to fear that they will. Their symptoms do not even have to show. They only have to think that there is a possibility of this happening for them to feel fearful and anxious.

2 *Exposure to the feared social situations almost invariably provokes anxiety.* The precise things that someone with

social phobia fears may be quite idiosyncratic: talking on the telephone, prolonging a conversation, entering a room full of people, eating or writing when other people can see what they are doing, or speaking up in front of a group of others; but having to do these things is nearly always difficult for them. Of course, there is no hard and fast line between normal and clinical levels of anxiety – all degrees of social anxiety exist – but social anxiety at a normal level is relatively intermittent. The feelings come and they also go. For everyone there are likely to be some particularly bad times, for example when starting a new job and going through the ordeal of showing that you can do what is expected of you. There are also likely to be some relatively good ones, when you feel more confident and at ease. For people whose level of social anxiety causes them to suffer there are more bad times and fewer good ones, and the bad times are worse.

3 *The person recognizes that the fear is excessive and unreasonable.* One of the distressing consequences of having a social phobia is that you know that the things that make you anxious are not really dangerous, and that they may hardly bother other people at all. But knowing that you suffer 'excessively' and 'unreasonably' compared with others – that in some sense the suffering is unnecessary – only makes it worse. It can make you feel unconfident, inadequate or inferior as well as anxious.

4 *The feared social or performance situations are avoided or else are endured with intense anxiety or distress.* It is only natural – it makes sense in terms of self-protection – to avoid or escape from frightening situations. The experience of

fear alerts you to the possibility of danger. Staying where you are might be risky. However, people with social anxiety are in an especially difficult position as they do not want to be lonely and isolated, and they cannot control the sources of their fear: other people and the thoughts that other people might have about them. Contact with people, when shopping, travelling or working, cannot be avoided completely, and socially anxious people want to work, make friends and feel that they belong just as much as others. So instead of avoiding or escaping from difficult situations, they may endure them despite the distress that they feel, and focus on keeping the risks or threats as small as possible: on keeping themselves as safe as they can. The intensity of the anxiety they feel makes this strategy seem only sensible.

In order to emphasize the difference between normal social anxiety and *social phobia*, the technical term for the clinical diagnosis, the diagnostic manual adds some general points: the problem must interfere with the person's life, cause a significant degree of distress and have persisted for at least six months. Whether or not these aspects of the problem are severe enough to fulfil criteria for social phobia is to some extent a matter of clinical judgment, as there is, for example no hard and fast way of deciding what degree of distress counts as significant.

For diagnostic purposes, two kinds of social phobia have been distinguished. For some people the problem is relatively limited and is confined to a few situations, such as speaking in public (the most common *specific social phobia*), or being with sexually attractive people; for others it is more likely to affect most situations involving interaction with others, and in these cases it is called *generalized social phobia*. In this book the term 'social anxiety' rather than 'social phobia' will be used, because there is no hard and fast distinction between being socially anxious and having a (diagnosable) social phobia; because social anxiety is what people with social phobia feel, so it makes sense to use the ordinary language term that refers to both conditions; and because the same ideas apply to understanding the problem and working out how to overcome it irrespective of whether you have mild, occasional social anxiety or a more entrenched and distressing social phobia.

Shyness is another term that could be used here, and people who are shy will recognize and understand many of the descriptions given above. The term has not been used so far for the sake of simplicity, but, as we shall see in the next chapter, shyness is similar to social anxiety, even though it is not a 'diagnosis'. More is known about social anxiety than about shyness, which psychologists have only recently started to study, but there is much overlap between the two, and the symptoms of social anxiety which are described in the next section of this chapter are also likely to be familiar to shy people. This does not mean that shy people should be 'diagnosed' as having a psychological disorder, but reflects the fact that shyness as well as social anxiety comes in varying degrees, and that its effects can be more or less problematic.

The symptoms of social anxiety

The technical definition of the problem provides a starting point for our understanding. The next step is to think about how social anxiety affects you. What are its main symptoms?

The four main types of symptoms are shown in Box 1.1, together with some examples. No two people are ever exactly the same and there are many possible symptoms, so if the ones you experience are not there, just add them to the list. In order to start making an assessment of the problem for yourself, think carefully about how your version of social anxiety affects your *thinking*, your *behavior*, your *body* and your *emotions*. It would be unusual not to have any symptoms at all in one of these four categories, although it can at first be difficult to recognize some of them in yourself. It is worth spending some time thinking through your particular experience of social anxiety, using this list as a prompt.

BOX 1.1: EXAMPLES OF THE SIGNS AND SYMPTOMS OF SOCIAL PHOBIA

Effects on thinking
- Worrying about what others think of you
- Finding it difficult to concentrate, or remember what people say
- Focusing attention on yourself; being painfully aware of what you do and say
- Thinking about what might go wrong, ahead of time
- Dwelling on things you think you did wrong, after the event
- Mind going blank; being unable to think what to say

Effects on behavior
- Speaking quickly or quietly, mumbling, getting words mixed up
- Avoiding catching someone's eye
- Doing things to make sure that you do not attract attention
- Keeping safe: in 'safe' places, or talking to 'safe' people, about 'safe' topics
- Avoiding difficult social occasions or situations

Effects on the body
- Signs of anxiety that others can see, such as blushing, sweating or trembling
- Feeling tense; the aches and pains that go with being unable to relax
- Panicky feelings: heart pounding, dizziness or nausea, breathlessness

Effects on emotions or feelings
- Nervousness, anxiety, fear, apprehension, self-consciousness
- Frustration and anger, with oneself and/or with others
- Feeling unconfident; feelings of inferiority
- Feeling sad, or depressed, or hopeless about being able to change

In practice the symptoms link up with each other, so that thoughts, behaviors, bodily reactions and emotions (or feelings) interlink in various ways, and each of them affects all of the others. For example, thinking you look foolish makes you feel self-conscious, so you look away, and try to fade into the background, which makes you aware that you are trembling and your heart is thumping. Or feeling hot and panicky makes it hard to think what to say, so you blurt out something that makes little sense, and then feel embarrassed. This interconnection between thoughts, feelings (both emotions and bodily feelings or sensations) and behavior makes it hard to disentangle how a particular bout of anxiety first started. Chapter 5 describes more about how the various aspects of social anxiety fit together.

Beyond the definition: What is it like to have this problem?

A definition and a list of symptoms provide the starting place for thinking about social anxiety, but they do not give the complete picture – or do justice to the suffering involved. It is hardly surprising that a problem that potentially affects so many aspects of life should have wide-ranging effects.

Subtle kinds of avoidance

Some socially anxious people avoid going out with friends, to meetings or to grander social occasions such as weddings, but many others continue to go to events that they fear, and on the surface it seems that their lives are not restricted and that avoidance is not a problem for them. However, this is to overlook the many subtle ways in which one can avoid difficult aspects of situations, some of which are shown in Box 1.2. If you avoid something you cannot learn that it is, despite what one might think about it, harmless. It is important not to overlook subtle kinds of avoidance as, like avoidance of any kind, they play an important part in keeping the problem going.

BOX 1.2: SUBTLE KINDS OF AVOIDANCE

- Waiting for someone else to arrive before entering a room full of people
- Handing things round at a party, so as to avoid getting into conversation
- Putting things off, such as meeting the neighbours or shopping at crowded times
- Turning away when you see someone coming who makes you feel anxious
- Avoiding talking about anything personal
- Avoiding using your hands when others might be watching
- Not eating in public places

Avoidance is not doing something because to do it would make you anxious.

Safety behaviors

Other people are the problem for people who are socially anxious, and one of the difficulties about other people is that you can never predict what they will do next. At any moment they may, unwittingly perhaps, 'land you in it': that is, they may do precisely the thing that you find hardest to deal with, such as put you on the spot by asking you a direct question; introduce you to the person who makes you feel most anxious (someone in authority or the most attractive person in the room); ask for your opinion; or just walk away from you to talk to someone else. So when with other people you can feel perpetually at risk – and it is not at all clear what you could avoid to make yourself feel better. Then your mind naturally focuses on how to keep safe. Socially anxious people develop a wide repertoire of 'safety behaviors', or things that they do in order to reduce the sense of being at risk: looking at the floor so that no one can catch their eye; wearing heavy make-up to hide their blushes, or light clothing in case they feel hot and sweaty; leaving the room immediately the meeting is over so that they do not have to get involved in 'small talk'. More examples of safety behaviors are shown in Box 1.3.

If you read through this list you will notice that some of them appear to be opposites, like either keeping quiet or trying to keep the conversation going. This is because different people want to do different things in order to feel safe. For some it feels safer to say little, and to make sure that what they do say makes sense. That way they feel as if they can reduce the risk of making fools of themselves. Others feel safer if they take responsibility for keeping a conversation going. When a silence feels like eternity it can feel safer to keep on chattering even if you might not be making a lot of sense.

BOX 1.3: EXAMPLES OF SAFETY BEHAVIORS

- Rehearsing what you are about to say; mentally checking you have got the words right
- Speaking slowly, or quietly; or talking fast and not stopping to draw breath
- Hiding your hands or face; putting your hand to your mouth
- Holding things tight, or locking your knees together to control shaking

- Letting your hair fall in front of your face; wearing clothes that hide parts of your body
- Trying to amuse people and tell jokes; or never risking a joke
- Not talking about yourself or your feelings; not expressing opinions
- Saying nothing that might be challenging or controversial; always agreeing
- Wearing smart clothes (the 'veneer'), or unnoticeable clothes (so as not to stand out)
- Sticking with a 'safe' person or in a 'safe' place; not taking any chances
- Keeping an eye on the escape route; never getting fully involved

A safety behavior is doing something to keep yourself safe. Many safety behaviors involve trying not to attract unwanted attention.

Dwelling on the problem

Social anxiety can come upon you, and feel overwhelming when it does, at the drop of a hat – partly because of the unpredictability of others, and partly because the fear of it is constantly in the mind. So *anticipatory anxiety* becomes part of the problem as well. Thinking about future encounters brings to mind a host of thoughts about how things might go wrong, often in rather vague and threatening ways: 'What if ... I can't think of anything to say? ... Everyone else knows people but I don't? ... I'm expected to speak up? ... My voice starts to tremble?' Apprehension and worry make it hard to look forw events, or aspects of them, that others enjoy or find relaxing such as the drink after the football game, the lunch break at work, going to a party or visiting a friend.

Even when the event is over the mind is prey to further anxiety, constantly turning over thoughts, images and memories of what happened, conducting the kind of post mortem that airport authorities might take part in after a 'near miss' on the runway. Socially anxious people tend to ruminate about aspects of their interactions with others that trouble them, as if they were narrowly averted catastrophes. They focus on something that they think they did 'wrong', or that did not feel quite right, or that embarrassed them, and they make assumptions about other people's reactions, including their private and unexpressed opinions. These assumptions place the socially anxious person in a negative light, so the postmortem after even a brief, uneventful interaction can bring on a bout of self-criticism: 'I'm hopeless – useless – too anxious to pay attention or think straight – stupid – different from everyone else – inept.' When it comes to being hard on themselves, the resourcefulness of people who suffer from social anxiety is almost limitless.

Of course, we all sometimes do something that embarrasses or humiliates us. We all have memories of a few things that make us cringe, blush, curl up or want to hide when we think of them, and remembering these things can bring back all the dreadful feelings with which one was engulfed at the time – even if it happens at four o'clock in

see the blushes. There is nothing
mortem itself – indeed, it prob-
process other intense or distressing
go over such things in our minds
e can assimilate them, adjust accord-
, leaving the distress behind. The post
mortem... ore a reflection of the suffering of social
phobias; but, s we shall see below, it perpetuates the
suffering rather than resolves it. The post mortems
conducted by people who suffer from social anxiety are
largely based on what they think happened, and not on
what actually happened; on what they think other people
thought of them rather than on what they actually thought.
They are unnecessary because they are based on guesswork, not fact.

Self-esteem, self-confidence and feelings of inferiority

Social anxiety makes you feel different from other people,
in a negative way – less good than them, or odd – and so
it comes to affect your self-esteem (sense of self-worth) as
well as your self-confidence (belief in your ability to do
things). You come to expect that people will ignore or reject
you, and tend to interpret the things that they do, like the
way they look at you or speak to you, as signs that they
think badly of you. You feel at risk of being on the receiving
end of their criticism or negative evaluation – of being found
wanting in some way – as if your weaknesses or inadequacies were about to be revealed. So you may live with a
constant undercurrent of fear, and with the sense that you

are lurching from one lucky escape to the next. Many socially anxious people think that others would reject them outright if they only knew what they were really like, and go to great lengths to hide their 'real selves', even though there is nothing wrong with them other than feeling anxious. Of course, this makes it hard to express an opinion or to say how they feel about something. They may also suppose that other people are never socially anxious; that they have fewer, or less socially revealing, weaknesses and inadequacies; or that they are able to go through life without feeling nervous about how others think of them. In fact it causes just as many problems to be impervious to others as it does to be too sensitive to them.

Demoralization and depression; frustration and resentment

It feels frustrating to stifle parts of your personality, so not surprisingly, persistent social anxiety gets you down. It can make you feel demoralized or depressed as well as anxious or angry, and resentful that others apparently find easy so many things that for you are seriously difficult. Anxiety is by no means the only emotion associated with social anxiety.

Effects on performance

The difficulty about high levels of anxiety – whatever causes them – is that they interfere with activities and with the ability to put plans into action. They make it harder for people to perform to the best of their abilities, and prevent them achieving the things that they want to achieve. A certain amount of anxiety is helpful if you have to go for an interview, or sit an examination: it can energize and motivate you, and help to focus your mind; but more than that becomes preoccupying and makes it hard to behave as you otherwise would, or hard to do your best. So in the short term social anxiety stops people doing what they want to do, and might otherwise be capable of doing, and in the long term this can have a wide range of different effects, on careers, personal relationships, friendships, work and leisure activities.

Varieties of social anxiety

Social anxiety may be limited to one main aspect of life, such as eating or speaking in public, or it may be more pervasive, and have more general effects. Some people cope reasonably well at work until they are offered the kind of promotion that would make them more 'visible', or require them to manage others. They might be unable to accept the promotion because it would involve attending meetings at which they would have to account for their department's activities or make presentations, or because they would have to attend a training course, or organize, oversee and take responsibility for the work of others. These people may refuse promotion and remain in jobs that are well below their capabilities, so that they fail to realize much of their potential.

Others are able to operate well at work, even in high-profile professional jobs or in ones that are socially demanding like being a salesperson or working in public relations. These people have few difficulties as long as they are 'protected' by the conventions that surround them in the workplace. They feel fine in the lab, computer room or operating theatre, but may still feel at a loss in unstructured social gatherings or when their role is not clearly defined, and find it difficult to make friends – and particularly difficult to make 'small talk'. Despite considerable success at work, they may still feel lonely and isolated, and their social anxiety means that sometimes they miss out on opportunities for forming close and intimate relationships as well.

Quite a number of people suffer severely from what has been called 'dating anxiety' – a degree of which is sufficiently common to be entirely normal – and they go through such agonies when with someone they find attractive that they become unable to put themselves across, or do those things that would help them to get to know the person they feel strongly about. Others may have one or two good friends, and feel comfortable most of the time within the circle of those that they know well: when with their partners, or surrounded by their families. For them social anxiety interferes with meeting new people, moving to new places, or seeking out new ways of fulfilling themselves, and their lives can become painfully limited and restricted. Social anxiety has many faces.

Some misconceptions

There are two other kinds of anxiety that might be thought to be kinds of social anxiety: performance anxiety and stage fright. In the case of performance anxiety, the factors that make someone vulnerable are to do with wanting to be able to produce their best performance – or at least a good one – when it really matters, and to come up to the mark in their own estimation. Other people's evaluation of the performance may therefore be less important to people with performance anxiety than their own evaluation of it, and they may be absolutely certain of their technique, and of their ability to produce a performance of the standard they wish, but fearful that the pressures of the actual performance will interfere with this ability.

Stage fright is probably a version of performance anxiety, and this sudden burst of fear can be totally paralyzing when it occurs, but it is specific to people who give public performances, and may occur in those who are otherwise socially confident only when they have to perform.

A related but contrary thought is that people who are able to give public performances, and actors in particular, are not socially anxious. The assumption is that they would never be able to forget themselves sufficiently to get up in front of other people, and put themselves on display, if doing so provoked catastrophic thoughts about what other people thought of them, and aroused all the signs and symptoms of anxiety that can be so distressing. But once again the assumption appears to be wrong: many actors, and others who provide different kinds of performances in public, may still be shy or anxious in other social situations, but able to hide their anxiety, or shyness, while 'in role'. They may also intentionally adopt a role, rather as others use safety behaviors, to help them out of a potential social difficulty.

How common is social phobia?

It is surprisingly difficult to estimate the frequency of problems such as social phobia accurately because, as will already be clear, the diagnosis is partly a matter of clinical judgment. The studies that are now available suggest that between 3 and 13 per cent of the population will suffer from sufficiently severe social anxiety to fulfil criteria for a diagnosis of social phobia at some time in their lives. The variation arises because the studies use slightly different methods and have been done at different times in different places. In most countries the problem appears to affect men and women equally often, though the precise form that it takes may differ between the sexes, partly depending on relevant cultural factors. For example, it used to be (and possibly still is) much harder for men than for women to seek help for psychological difficulties, and easier for men than for women to use alcohol to boost their social courage. Many specialists in treatment of alcohol-related problems have observed that social anxiety appears to contribute to the development of these problems. People report drinking, or using other substances, to reduce the anxiety they experience socially, and when problems with addiction resolve, the social anxiety may remain, or re-emerge. There are probably many ways of masking a problem of social anxiety, and of course the anxiety itself makes people reluctant to talk about the problem, so our present estimates of frequency may be too low.

It is interesting, for example, that 40 per cent of the adult population of America describe themselves as 'shy', even though we are not quite sure what they might mean by this. They could be referring to normal levels of social anxiety, to a subjective impression of sensitivity in the presence of others, to their memory of the normal stage of shyness through which most children pass and to its occasional shadow in adult life, or to something else such as feeling generally unconfident. But we do know that shyness is more common than social anxiety, and the nature and effects of shyness are described in more detail in the next chapter.

Cultural variation

Social anxiety is found all over the world. Undoubtedly its nature varies a bit with local customs, but people everywhere can worry about the possibility of doing something that might be embarrassing or humiliating for them. Exactly what that will be depends on where they are, whom they are with and the conventions that have grown up in that place at that time. What might be thought of as hot-headed displays of emotion are common in Mediterranean countries and relatively rare in Nordic ones, where they might be misunderstood or attract unwanted attention. Behaviors that would provoke feelings of shame in Japan might go unnoticed in America, and vice versa. For example, making too much eye contact too soon can be embarrassing in Japan, whereas for an American person not looking directly at the person to whom you are talking, especially if you have just met them, or if they are in some way important to you, might suggest that you have something to hide. The point is that there is no single set of social conventions but many different 'socially acceptable' ways of behaving, depending on where you are. Even in the same place, these will differ depending on whether you are 18 or 80.

KEY POINTS

- It is normal occasionally to feel socially anxious. Indeed, this seems to be a universal phenomenon.
- People for whom social anxiety causes problems suppose that other people are evaluating them negatively, and fear that they will do something in public that will be embarrassing or humiliating.
- There are four different kinds of symptoms: these affect thinking, behavior, the body, and emotions or feelings.
- Socially anxious people avoid difficult situations, try to keep themselves safe, worry about what might happen before the event and about what did happen afterwards, and may feel angry, depressed or inferior as well as anxious.
- Social anxiety can interfere with all aspects of life: professional as well as personal.
- The exact form that it takes varies from person to person, from place to place and from time to time.
- There is no need to know exactly what caused it in order to be able to change.

2

About shyness

Describing shyness and its effects is different from describing social anxiety because shyness is not a diagnosis, and there are no agreed criteria of shyness to use as starting points for a technical definition. Nevertheless, in some ways shyness may be easier to understand than social anxiety or social phobia because it is so common, especially in adolescence and early adulthood. Most people have been through stages of shyness, often of an extremely painful nature, and know, or can easily remember, the fear and trepidation with which they approached all sorts of social situations when feeling shy. Shyness has recently been studied in more detail, mostly in America, and the findings from these studies provide much useful information about the nature of shyness and its effects. Some of the findings from this research are described here.

Facts and figures about shyness

Statistics gathered by research teams have found that only about 5 per cent of adults believe they have never been shy at all, and about 80 per cent of people say that they experienced periods of pronounced shyness during childhood and adolescence. It seems that about half the people who were shy when they were young grow out of the problem to a large degree, though a sizeable proportion of them remain shy in some situations. About 40 per cent of adults in America still describe themselves as shy, and in California there is some recent evidence that this number is slowly increasing. Shyness, it appears, is not dying away, but on the contrary is posing more people problems than it used to.

Although the reasons for this increase are not properly understood yet, there has been some interesting speculation about the factors in modern life that could contribute to such a change. For example, it has been suggested that people get less practice nowadays at certain kinds of social interactions than they used to. Many activities that once depended on direct communication with someone else, such as withdrawing money from a bank, filling the car up with petrol and making a complicated telephone call, can now be carried out successfully without interacting directly with anyone else. Buying groceries usually involves consulting a mental (or real) list while filling up a trolley rather than asking someone to find the things on the list for you and creating an opportunity to carry on a conversation, and develop a relationship, with the person supplying the goods you need.

At work, many people spend much of their day, whether they are carrying out complex business transactions or routine, repetitive tasks, face to face with a computer screen rather than another person. Business and social interactions, including making contact with people who have similar interests, or even just chatting, can be conducted using a keyboard, screen and mouse – on the Web or the Net or in cyberspace – with no social content of the kind that helps people to overcome their initial shyness and to develop their confidence when meeting people face to face. Such interactions also obey completely different sets of conventions about how to communicate, which require specific skills and knowledge of new 'languages'. Although these new methods of communication are in some ways extremely successful (fascinating and seductive too), there are many things that they do not demand, like being polite or friendly, or sensitive to how someone else is feeling and how their feelings change. They do not require their users to be aware of what might lie behind the communications they receive, or of what it means to others to be in contact with you. Nor do they have to be able to laugh with you, or look at you. For someone who feels shy or wary about doing these things, or who fears that they might be being evaluated or judged or criticized when they do, this may be a relief. It is unlikely that using a computer would make someone self-conscious – that is, unless they were being watched as they used it.

These changes are a product of technological advances which tend to leave those who do not keep up with them in a different world from those who do. But instead of creating a social cohesion and ease of communication between the people 'in the know', they leave the users of the common system isolated, in social terms, from each other – able to have 'virtual' rather than real conversations.

The communication may well succeed in its own way, and is often interesting and enjoyable, but it leaves people short of practice when it comes to picking up the subtle cues and nuances with which face-to-face interactions with people are filled, and from which social confidence grows.

Of course, the contribution of technology to changing patterns of shyness may be exaggerated, and other factors may also be at work; but the important point to remember is that shyness is the norm rather than the exception in early life, and that somewhere in the process of growing up, it normally lessens. It affects nearly everyone to some degree in early childhood, but continues to affect less than half the adult (American) population. So there are highly likely to be some things that can hasten this change, and others – like using electronic means of communication – that might delay it; and learning more about what shyness is, and about its effects, is likely to be helpful.

Is shyness a form of social anxiety, or is it something different?

A simple answer to this question is that there appear to be both similarities and differences between shyness and social anxiety, but the two types of social difficulty have not been studied equally long, and some of the finer points have yet to be elucidated. So this is a question that you may have to answer for yourself, by reading through this chapter and the previous one and thinking about the precise form that your problem takes.

Shyness has been said to run the whole gamut from mild

social awkwardness to extreme forms of withdrawal and inhibition that are indistinguishable from social phobia. However, one of the main differences between people who are shy and people who are socially anxious appears to be that, at least for a proportion of people, shyness can be a passing phenomenon. It can last for a few months or years in childhood, it can re-emerge during adolescence, or it can continue in an intermittent way, so that, for example, it disappears once the 'warm-up' phase in a relationship or interaction is over. Many people who are shy to start with experience little or no social anxiety once they have overcome their initial reticence.

Symptoms of shyness

Shyness appears always to involve a sense of shrinking back from social encounters, and of retreating into oneself. Perhaps for this reason, the main symptoms of shyness are closely similar to those of social anxiety described in the previous chapter. They include physical and psychological discomfort, inhibition, excessive self-focus, and being preoccupied with thoughts, feelings and physical reactions. Subjectively this may translate into a powerful sense of doing things wrong, as if everyone else knew what was required of them and knew how to decode the signals correctly. It can leave people feeling exposed, dreading the next moment, full of nervous tension, unable to forget the thumping heartbeat and the hot, red face. The predominant beliefs of shy people reflect this sense of vulnerability, and are of being – or of being judged by others to be –

inadequate, unlovable or unattractive. The way in which others react to shyness can make a difference to the symptoms too, as the more it appears to bother them, the longer it may last and the worse it may feel.

Shyness is most likely to be a problem in two types of situation: when interacting with people in a position of authority, and in one-to-one situations, especially when these involve talking to a sexually attractive person. Shy people usually become more vulnerable to their symptoms as the intimacy of a relationship increases, when they find that they are expected to initiate activities for a group of people, or when they wish to assert themselves. This is particularly likely to be a difficulty if they are feeling angry or irritated, as shy people generally prefer to avoid having overt disagreements, and may be uncertain of their ability to control their feelings (positive or negative) once they start to allow them full expression.

There are some grounds for making a distinction between two slightly different kinds of shyness. The first of these is the sense of wariness that children start to show with strangers at a very young age. It makes good sense, in evolutionary terms, to be wary of strangers, and this could be one contributory reason why the childhood form of shyness is so common, and so universal. It occurs in all cultures, and there seems to be no way of preventing it happening, nor indeed any need to prevent it happening. Most children outgrow this kind of shyness, at least to a large extent, and it is possible that people who do not have sufficient opportunity during childhood to find out how to interact with strangers, and to learn how to work out whether they are 'safe' or 'dangerous', take longer to do this than others. Obviously there are family resemblances at work here too, and in Chapter 4 there is a more detailed discussion of the many factors that contribute to causing social anxiety and shyness.

The second form of shyness is apparently more closely related to social anxiety, as its main features are described as inhibition and concern about being evaluated or judged by other people. It is possible that this form, as it is rooted in sensitivity to the perceived opinion of other people, develops later and is more likely to occur in those people for whom the 'wariness' form of shyness is slow to recede. However we do not as yet know whether most shy people suffer from both kinds of shyness, and nor do we know enough about the normal course of these forms of shyness, especially in people who subsequently suffer from social anxiety or social phobia, to be able to judge whether this distinction is a useful one, in the practical sense that it helps to work out how to overcome forms of shyness that continue to pose problems later in life.

Shyness and introversion

The wariness and inhibition that are predominant features of shyness should not be confused with introversion. Introverts are people who prefer solitary to social activities. They do not seek out the excitement of social interactions so often as extroverted people do, but find satisfaction in activities in which they can absorb themselves regardless of whether they have someone to interact with at the time. Introverts differ from people who are socially anxious in that social life is not something that makes them fearful and nervous so much as something that plays a different part in their lives. Introverts can form close friendships and make intimate relationships without particular difficulty when they are interested in doing so, and they seek out solitude and opportunities for independent activity not because they are lonely or isolated but because that is their style.

This means that shy people, and socially anxious ones too, may be either introverted or extroverted. Their natural style may be more or less sociable, and the form that the problem takes may be somewhat different depending on what they would really prefer their social life to be like. For a shy extrovert it may be relatively easy to become engaged in sociable activities that are well structured, so that they know what is expected of them and are less fearful of doing something 'wrong', and relatively difficult to become involved in more intimate or less structured situations. Paradoxically perhaps, a shy person who is introverted may suffer less than a shy extrovert, as many of the activities that they enjoy and find satisfying can be carried out alone.

The effects of shyness

The main effects of shyness as reported in the studies available so far are similar to the main effects of social anxiety. They are summarized in Box 2.1.

BOX 2.1: THE MAIN EFFECTS OF SHYNESS

(Note the similarities with Box 1.1 on page 9.)

- Self-consciousness and self-awareness
- Thoughts about being evaluated negatively, and of being judged or criticized
- Beliefs about being inadequate, unlovable or unattractive
- Avoidance and withdrawal; a sense of inward shrinking; not getting involved
- Finding it hard to take the initiative or to be assertive
- Feeling anxious, apprehensive, frustrated or unhappy
- Physical symptoms such as blushing and other signs of nervousness

NB: Shy people are NOT less attractive, less intelligent or less competent than other people, but they may think that they are.

In addition, shyness can have some indirect effects. For example, when feeling shy, people can become so self-conscious and preoccupied with themselves and their feelings that they are no longer able to pay proper attention to their surroundings or to what they are doing. That is when they cover themselves with confusion by doing something clumsy like knocking over a drink, or stumbling over a step, or bumping into a chair or table. Shy people are normally no more clumsy than anyone else, but they become so, much to their chagrin, at the worst possible times for them, when they least want to draw attention to themselves and would far prefer to appear less awkward than they feel.

It is interesting that shy children suffer fewer disadvantages from their shyness than one might expect. Their self-esteem remains unaffected at first, and so does their ability to form friendships. However, when shyness continues then the problem appears to interfere more with their lives, so that adults who have always been shy more frequently end up doing jobs that they do not enjoy, or that fail to allow them to take full advantage of their potential, or that earn less money, than people who have succeeded in overcoming their childhood shyness. As a consequence perhaps, many of them do suffer later on from lowered self-esteem, and a few also from another secondary effect of long-lasting shyness that may be rather surprising. They tend to have more problems with their physical health than might otherwise be expected.

It has been suggested that this is because their shyness makes it hard for them to confide in others and to talk about their personal problems, or things that many people are sensitive or easily embarrassed about. Therefore they may receive less professional advice than they need, and less support from the people around them when something stressful or distressing happens to them. Psychological research tells us that having a good support network, and being able to express feelings, whether face to face with someone else or in some other way such as by writing or through music, poetry or physical activity, for example, helps people to overcome all sorts of problems. Self-expression helps people recover more quickly than keeping things to oneself, and that means that people who are able to do this suffer less from the fatigue that usually goes with persistent stress or distress, and apparently also become less vulnerable to minor illnesses.

Shame and blame

Many shy people feel ashamed of themselves for being shy – as if it were their fault, and they were to blame for not having overcome the problem – despite in most cases persisting in doing things that they find difficult, and even waging a determined campaign against it. Just like people who are socially anxious, they tend to ignore or discount their successes, and to think of times when things went well for them socially as lucky escapes. They remember, and tend to dwell on, any information that fits with their sense of being awkward or inadequate. Shy people are likely to interpret ambiguous remarks made to them or about them, such as 'You seem to be rather quiet', as if they were criticisms, and they remember such remarks better than people who are not shy. They go through life expecting other people to be critical of them, and if they are asked to describe themselves they come up with more negative and fewer positive judgments than other people would.

Advantages of shyness

Given the wide-ranging effects of shyness it may seem surprising that it also has some substantial advantages. Shyness is an attractive quality to many people. It can be difficult to get to know someone who is shy, but the difficulty, far from putting people off, can make people interested to know more, as if there were a mystery to be solved, and the process of getting to know a shy person held unexpected rewards. The sense of someone gradually warming to the attention they are given, and opening up as they begin to feel more confident, can make the friend who is giving the attention feel that they have won a valued confidence, and it can also make them feel good about themselves, for example for being sensitive and attentive. Shyness is closely related to that much-admired characteristic of the British: reserve, and it can go with a becoming form of modesty that is contrary to some characteristics that are not so universally admired, such as arrogance, loudness, being self-opinionated, pushy or conceited.

So another view is that there is nothing inherently wrong with shyness – and indeed some people quite consciously take advantage of the fact that it can be a most attractive quality, and use their shyness (real or 'enhanced', perhaps) as a means of making people curious about them. Shyness can be an invitation, used to draw people in: a clue that there are hidden qualities to be discovered, or a mystery to be unravelled. People take advantage of their shyness in various ways and may be accused, if they flutter their eyelashes too much, of being manipulative when they do so, though often the intention is not to produce a desired reaction in someone else so much as to give themselves a helping hand in picking up the social cues or clues in a new or unfamiliar situation. Being shy, and holding back until you feel confident enough to join in, is safer than being bold or uninhibited, especially if you fear doing the wrong thing socially and need time to get your social bearings – so that you can, for example, find out who is who and how you should react to them, and avoid committing the *faux pas* of sitting in someone else's place, or finishing up the last of the strawberries.

It is also possible that having too little shyness in one's make-up might be just as bad as having too much. A certain amount of shyness may apply the brakes on putting oneself forward, particularly in situations in which one person finds another attractive, and wants to make this clear irrespective of whether their attentions are welcomed, or regardless of the appropriateness of doing so at that time or in that place. The ability to turn a social contact into a 'real', emotional connection, and, for example, to make people laugh or to tell jokes, is almost universally valued socially; but it is still important to be able to judge what is appropriate when. People who do not suffer from shyness at all may not pay attention to such considerations, and say or do some 'outrageous' things which can be so embarrassing to people who are shy that they can hardly bear to be near them – or even to watch them on the television. A balance between inhibition and disinhibition may lead to least social difficulty – though it must also be admitted that having disinhibited people around can make for a good party, and that having inhibited ones around can introduce a valuable sensitivity to others, as well as a note of caution that may (or may not) be so valuable.

Shyness and rudeness

It is clear that the fear of intruding and of giving offence, or of being rude, has something to do with shyness. Shy people often find it hard to ask questions, and of course there are many ways in which asking questions might be intrusive or offensive, so they provide a good focus for the discussion at this point. Questions can be nosy or inquisitive. They can be too personal, or a product of idle curiosity, or they can make someone feel that they are being interrogated. Some questions are clearly rude: 'How did you get so rich?' 'Why is he so fat?', and children learn remarkably quickly to stifle them, despite their understandable curiosity.

What makes questions so risky – especially for people who are shy? One answer to this question is that they are extremely useful socially, but they also run the risk of appearing rude. One of the main ways in which people find out about each other is by asking questions, but the conventions about what is acceptable and what is not vary. In order to develop the manners and the sensitivity that fit with the culture one is in, one has to be sensitive to these conventions. So during childhood we all learn a large number of social rules, for example about not interrupting, or talking too much about ourselves, or upsetting other people, and we also learn that it is wrong, embarrassing and even unacceptable, to do these or similar things. However, as conventions vary, even between people who share the same background but are of different ages, it is always possible to be rude by mistake. Perhaps shy people become overconcerned about making mistakes and about their consequences, so that to them social life feels rather like finding their way through a minefield of potentially explosive devices. Perhaps mistakes have too much significance for them, as if being (unintentionally) rude makes them inadequate, or unacceptable, or likely to be rejected. Or perhaps such mistakes did on occasion have dire consequences as they were growing up.

Knowing the rules about what is rude and what is not is certainly helpful, but we all receive messages as children that are hard to fit together, such as 'Look at me when I'm talking to you' and 'Don't look at me like that', so knowing the rules is never enough. There are always exceptions, and they often have to be adapted to particular circumstances; shyness makes people uncertain about how to adapt, and makes them feel too inhibited to attempt to do things differently. When this happens, misunderstandings can easily arise. For example, one person thinks, 'If he wanted me to know, then he would tell me,' and does not ask questions because of not wanting to intrude. But the other person thinks, 'She never asks, so she's not interested' and both of them keep quiet when that is not what either of them really wants.

It is likely that the minefield can be negotiated more easily by learning to be sensitive to other people. Learning to pick up the signals, and learning how to repair the damage when one has done something 'wrong', are important tasks, and neither of these can be done so well when feeling self-conscious. The self-awareness and self-focused attention of shy and socially anxious people may make them less aware of others and more at risk of giving offence by mistake. But at the same time, feeling shy or socially anxious makes it seem especially important not to be rude or to give offence. So shy and socially anxious people appear to be caught both ways.

Cultural variations

Shyness appears to occur everywhere in the world, but not to the same degree. Of course, no one has yet collected information about the forms of shyness present in every single country and culture in the world, but nevertheless some generalizations are starting to emerge. For example, among young adults shyness appears to affect only about one-third of the people in Israel but nearly two-thirds of those in Japan.

Within each culture gender differences appear to be absent, suggesting that shyness affects men and women equally. However, culturally there are differences in the ways in which people understand and react to shyness in men and in women. It is generally considered to be a more feminine than masculine trait, and to be more acceptable in women than in men. Shy middle-aged women may remain shy but no longer find that this causes them any problems if they live a rather traditional, family-oriented life, focused on a local, well-known community. But shy men develop, and keep on using, more ways of concealing their shyness from others. They learn how to hide behind the 'rules of the game', or the structure required by their work or business situations, and to adopt the roles needed for the functions they perform without involving themselves personally. People everywhere, and of both sexes, know that having a drink can make them feel less inhibited socially, and shy people as well as socially anxious ones use alcohol to help them feel better, in an attempt to boost their confidence.

Implications

Clearly, shyness and social anxiety are close relatives. There is much overlap in their symptoms and in their effects, and there are many reasons to suppose that the strategies that have been shown to be helpful in overcoming social anxiety are also valuable for overcoming shyness. In the rest of this book the term *social anxiety* will be used instead of saying *social anxiety and shyness* each time; it will be assumed that the ideas apply to shyness as well as to social anxiety throughout. In particular, all the strategies for overcoming the problems will be described in such a way that they make sense whether you see your version of the problem as predominantly one or the other.

KEY POINTS

- Shyness is almost universal, although about half the people who suffer from it in childhood overcome the problem as adults.
- The symptoms of shyness are similar to those of social anxiety.
- Shyness is different from introversion. Introverted people have a less sociable style than extroverted ones, and shy people may be either introverts or extroverts.
- The effects of shyness are wide-ranging, similar to those of social anxiety, and extend to all aspects of life, professional as well as personal.
- Shyness has advantages as well as disadvantages, and can be an attractive characteristic. Our social life probably benefits from having the full range of people in it: shy or inhibited as well as bold or disinhibited.
- Shy people often fear being rude, or giving offence, and are careful not to do this by mistake.
- There are probably some cultural differences in shyness, but few differences between the frequency of the problem in men and in women.
- The term *social anxiety* will be used from now on to refer to shyness as well.

3

Is social anxiety all in the mind? The central role of thinking in social anxiety

Social anxiety is rooted in thoughts. Socially anxious people think that others think badly of them, or that they are judging them – hence the potential for humiliation and embarrassment. To make matters worse, they think that the things that they suppose other people are thinking are true. 'They don't want me with them.' 'They think I'm weird.' 'They don't like me.' Underneath they may believe that they are different or odd and don't quite belong, or that they are certain to do something embarrassing or inept; to reveal their inadequacies or to be rejected, even if they have not put these beliefs into words. Of course the fear, anxiety and distress of social anxiety are closely linked to such thoughts, and to the meaning that having such thoughts has.

So thinking plays a central part in social anxiety, and understanding this part of the problem is essential in working out how exactly to overcome it. The main idea – and this is also the main idea behind the development of cognitive behavior therapy (CBT) – is that what you think affects what you feel (and of course what you do as well). Thinking can trigger bouts of anxiety ('I'm making a complete idiot of myself') and it can keep the anxiety going once it has started. Thinking 'I can't think of anything to say', or 'They're all going to judge me, and criticize me for being so idiotic', will only prolong the bad feelings, and influence how you behave when you are with other people. In addition, the attitudes, beliefs and assumptions that people have can make them more or less vulnerable to social anxiety in the first place: 'I'm just not acceptable as I am'; 'Anybody I like wouldn't like me'; 'I'm different, or odd'. So the many ways that people think contribute to the development and to the maintenance of their anxiety, and if they could only change the way that they think, then they would be likely to change their feelings and their behavior as well. This chapter is about how to understand the part played by thinking in social anxiety.

What do we mean by thinking?

Thoughts do not come like sentences, with capital letters at the beginning and full stops at the end. It is just that when we talk about them we usually express them in sentences. Some thoughts are relatively easy to identify, for example, 'They're all looking at me' or 'I'm not doing this right', and some are much harder, partly because they go without saying: for example, knowing that I'm just not 'up to it'. Indeed, some of the things that we think – or that we know or remember – are extremely difficult to put into words. Thoughts, or *cognitions*, include many things that go on in the mind as well as straightforward thoughts: for example, attitudes, ideas and expectations; memories, impressions and images; and beliefs and assumptions. Our vocabulary gives us many words for referring to the contents of our minds. Some of these types of cognition are obvious and easy to recognize, while others are harder, and one way of making sense of the relationship between thoughts and feelings is to define different levels of cognition: the level of attention, the level of automatic thoughts, and a deeper level of underlying beliefs and assumptions. These will be described next, before giving some attention to the special part that images can play in social anxiety.

The level of attention

First, social anxiety affects what you notice – what you pay attention to.

> When Judy was talking to her boss, Michael, she suddenly felt hot and sweaty. She was sure she was going red, and wanted to hide her face. She noticed that he seemed rather distant, but was puzzled by this. She had not properly heard what he had said, and wondered what she had done wrong.
>
> Don was listening to the banter going on between two workmates at the next bench. He noticed them glance his way, and felt himself withdrawing inside, seeking protection inside his 'shell'. He became preoccupied with

the fear that they were going to say something to him.
He felt too nervous and shaky to think of anything to
say back to them, especially anything amusing or witty,
and he was worried about what they thought about him
for not being able to join in.

As soon as they became anxious, Judy and Don both noticed the things that went on inside them, their internal sensations of blushing or wanting to withdraw. They both found it difficult to engage with what was going on around them, and focused their attention on their own concerns rather than those of the people with them. Once it was all over, it was easier to remember how bad and how foolish they felt than it was to remember exactly what anyone else had said or done.

These examples show how social anxiety focuses people's attention on themselves, and how *self-focused attention* makes people feel increasingly self-conscious. When we are socially anxious we can become painfully aware of ourselves and of our perceived shortcomings. It is difficult to forget the trembling hands or the glowing face once the trembling or blushing has begun, and once you start thinking about them they tend to dominate, so there is less attention left over for anything else. In the examples above, Judy thought she must have missed something that her boss Michael had said, and Don had no idea what his colleagues were really talking about when he noticed them glancing in his direction, or what they did next, once he had withdrawn into his shell. All he could remember was their tone of voice.

Of course, both Judy and Don noticed the people around them first. Indeed, they both tended to keep on the lookout for the types of situations that they found threatening, watching out for any dangers that they might be able to avoid. This *hypervigilance* is part of a natural mechanism for keeping safe, that directs attention towards potential threats, so the things that Judy and Don paid attention to were linked to their particular kind of fear: to their *social* anxiety. Judy felt socially inferior and inadequate, and was especially uncomfortable talking to people in authority over her. What she noticed was that Michael seemed rather distant, and this made her wonder what she might have done wrong. Don felt socially inept, and thought that other people found him too serious and slow-witted. What he noticed was the bantering tone of the conversation nearby, and the glance in his direction.

What people pay attention to determines what gets into their minds. When people are socially anxious their attention is more self-focused, they are hypervigilant for threats, and they notice and remember things that fit with their fears.

The level of automatic thoughts

Everything that happens to us makes us think. Even though we might not be aware of doing so, we are thinking all the time, and the things that we think reflect the ways in which we interpret, or appraise, the things that happen to us and around us. Sometimes our appraisals will be accurate, sometimes they will be overoptimistic, as if we saw the world through rose-tinted spectacles, and sometimes they will be overpessimistic, as if we saw only the negative possibilities. So when a stranger smiles at me I can think (accurately) that they are being friendly, optimistically that they think I look wonderful, and pessimistically that they can see I am feeling uncomfortable and are just trying to be kind. When people are anxious they tend to have a negative bias and to interpret things in terms of threats, as if the world were full of dangerous risks, and as if their resources were inadequate for dealing with these risks. *Negative automatic thoughts*, or *NATs*, predominate in their thinking. Examples of the kinds of NATs found in social anxiety are shown in Box 3.1.

BOX 3.1: EXAMPLES OF NEGATIVE AUTOMATIC THOUGHTS (NATs) IN SOCIAL ANXIETY

- I'll look foolish
- They think I'm . . . stupid . . . no good . . . boring
- I'll lose control of myself, and my anxiety will show
- Everyone is looking at me
- I don't belong
- They can see how nervous I am
- I can't concentrate, or think straight
- Everything I say is nonsense
- This is terrible: a complete disaster
- They don't like me
- I'm always doing things wrong

The level of underlying beliefs and assumptions

These reflect patterns of thinking and relatively permanent rules for living, or attitudes. Normally there is not much need for people to put their beliefs and assumptions into words. If you believe that most people are honest and trustworthy, then there is usually no need to say so unless you have a good reason to do so. This might happen if you were suddenly in doubt, or if you were asked specifically for your opinion. For instance, if you had to write a reference for someone then you might think about it properly, and make an attempt to put your impressions into words. In doing so you would probably draw on many things that you know and could remember about that person's character, their behavior, their way of talking to people, attitudes, history and so on.

Beliefs and assumptions about people are built up on a large body of information: direct experience, observation, information from others, how you feel about them, what you have learned, what you can remember, what you know about others like them and much else besides. Some of it will fit with being honest and trustworthy, but some of it might not fit. Underlying beliefs and assumptions convey basic, and usually unspoken, attitudes and overall impressions, and they are often quite hard to phrase in precisely the way that feels right.

This is hard enough when you are thinking about someone else and trying to be objective, as when writing a reference. It can be even harder when thinking about yourself. This is partly because it is easy to be swayed by subjective impressions, and partly because we all tend to approach the world, and to deal with the experiences that come our way, using our beliefs and assumptions as a guiding framework. The beliefs provide the shade of the glass in the spectacles through which we look out on the world, and the assumptions provide us with rules for living based on those beliefs. So if you believe that people are basically fair-minded you might assume that 'if you treat people right they will do the same by you'. If you believe that other people are basically hostile or critical you might assume that 'if you reveal too much about yourself, then others will discover your weaknesses and exploit them'.

Examples of beliefs and assumptions that are common in people with social anxiety are shown in Box 3.2. The beliefs are statements about the way things 'are', or seem to be. They reflect opinions and attitudes about yourself ('I always do the wrong thing'), about other people ('Other people always seem to know what to do'), and about the way things are in the world in general: 'terrible things can happen at the drop of a hat'. All three types of belief, about yourself, about other people and about the world, have a major impact on what you think, feel and do, and therefore on the ways in which you interact with the others around you. So they are relevant when social anxiety becomes a problem, as you will see by reading through the items listed in the box. Some of the beliefs in the box are like variations on a theme, and they have been presented like this because although people have similar beliefs, the precise way in which they would put them into words if they had to do so would vary considerably from person to person.

BOX 3.2: EXAMPLES OF BELIEFS AND ASSUMPTIONS

Beliefs

- I'm . . . odd . . . weird . . . different . . . boring . . . stupid . . . unatractive
- I'm inferior . . . inadequate . . . unacceptable . . . unlikeable
- I can't change . . . I'm stuck . . . there's no hope for me
- Nobody I like would like me
- Others don't like people who are . . . nervous . . . anxious . . . quiet . . . shy
- People are always judging me . . . criticizing . . . looking out for things I do wrong
- There is a right way of doing things
- It is wrong to break social rules and conventions

Assumptions

- I must be amusing and interesting or people won't like me
- If I am alone I am bound to be unhappy
- You've got to do things right if you're going to be acceptable
- If others want to know me they'll let me know
- If the conversation doesn't go well it is my fault
- People will take advantage of me if I show signs of weakness

The assumptions are like rules for living, and they are closely related to the strategies that people use to cope with their social anxiety. If you assume that it is your fault when a conversation goes badly then you will try to make sure that none of the conversations you are involved in are bad ones. Whether you do this by avoiding as many conversations as possible, or by trying to say exactly the right thing, or by planning what to say in advance, or by making sure that you always let the other person take the lead without imposing your ideas, or in yet another way will depend on you. People with closely similar assumptions may adopt different strategies for dealing with the same type of problem – and, as we saw earlier, they also adopt different strategies for keeping themselves safe.

Images in social anxiety

The tendency to think in images varies from person to person. Some people do not use imagery much, while others seem to use imagery all the time, and can summon up visual pictures of the things that happened to them almost as if they were turning on a video machine. Sometimes these images are purely visual, but sometimes they include sound or other sensory impressions as well, as if all the senses could contribute to the image that remains. This is true of everyone, whether or not they suffer from social anxiety.

Images have an extraordinarily immediate quality. They seem to encapsulate an enormous amount of information in a most efficient way, with the result that they often provoke strong feelings. Images also come and go quickly – sometimes so quickly that people are not aware of having them until they stop and ask themselves, or stop and think about it.

Sometimes, when people suddenly notice a change in their feelings that they are unable to understand or to explain, thinking about whether they had any images provides the explanation they were looking for. For example, a socially anxious woman who suddenly felt nervous when asked a question by an older man only realized later that her nervousness was triggered by an image of herself blushing in answer to an embarrassing personal question asked her by an uncle. This had happened at a family party when, in the hearing of many people, he had inquired teasingly about her relationship with someone he assumed (wrongly) was her boyfriend. When she denied there was anything special about the relationship, he continued to tease her, implying that she was not telling the truth and was too embarrassed to admit to it. Something that the two situations had in common appeared to have made the image pop into her mind again, and with it came all the nervousness and embarrassment that the first situation had originally provoked in her.

It is common for images to be based, like this one, on specific memories, and they may have a strong and immediate effect on the way you feel even if the memories are not clear and precise, but are more like overall impressions. So the impression of looking foolish in front of the class at school, or of being wrongly criticized and blamed for something, may leave behind a vivid image, and the image may come to mind in various situations later on, all of which are related in some way to the original situation. For example, the same image, or impression, may come to mind in situations that produce the same sorts of feelings, or in situations that have some of the same external characteristics, such as someone speaking in the same tone of voice, or saying some of the same words, or looking like the person who first provoked those feelings.

When people have images involving themselves, their position in the image can be represented in one of two ways: they may be looking at it from the outside in, so to speak, as if they could see themselves from someone else's point of view, or from the inside out, as if they were looking at the situation in which they find themselves through their own eyes. Seeing things from the inside, looking outwards, focuses attention on other people, and provides the right conditions for gathering accurate information about them: about their feelings and reactions, about whether they were listening, paying attention, interested in what was happening and so on.

But socially anxious people more often report having images of the first kind – seeing things from the outside in – than other people do. In their images they often see themselves as they assume others would see them. If they feel hot and bothered, then in their images they see themselves as looking hot and bothered (even if in reality their feelings were totally invisible to others). This has a number of effects. First, it makes them feel worse, as they become increasingly aware of the way they feel, and how that must look to others. Second, becoming more aware of their appearance, even if they are quite wrong about it, makes them feel more self-conscious. Third, the preoccupation with themselves makes it hard to pay attention to others, and to be sure about what is really going on, or what it means; and fourth, the image reflects what the socially anxious person fears rather than reality. If they fear looking stupid, then that is the way they see themselves in the image. As images are such efficient ways of conveying meaning, the image has an immediate impact, even if it is only fleeting. An image of looking stupid might, for example, mean that everyone can spot their weaknesses right away, and that they are basically socially inadequate. In this way, images appear to confirm underlying beliefs, even though in reality all they can do is reflect and reveal them.

This kind of socially anxious imagery helps to explain the symptoms and one of the ways in which they can suddenly increase, and when overcoming the problem it helps to learn how consciously to control imagery, and to explore ways of taking a different perspective. This could involve, for example, constructing and searching for images and memories of competent and effective interactions, and of situations seen the other way round, from the inside out, so as to pay better attention to other people and the details of the social event in question.

The meaning of social situations

From the examples above it is clear that the mind makes links between events with similar meanings, and that images may convey these meanings most efficiently. Images, after all, are internally generated, and the power that generates them, and influences the form that they take, is internal. Images are formed in the context of particular beliefs and assumptions, and they reflect these beliefs (the cognitive framework with which we approach the world) in pictures or in words, or in other more symbolic ways, as in dreams. For example, having a fleeting image of a moment when you floundered for words, and everything you said seemed to be muddled and confused, may carry with it various meanings, such as 'I always make myself look stupid', or 'I'm no good at talking to people', or 'No one would want much to do with me'. Indeed, often it is the meaning something has that is the most important cognitive part of it, and produces the strongest feelings. It is the meaning that is encapsulated in the beliefs about themselves, about other people and about the world that socially anxious people express, and these beliefs are quite literally reflected in the images that come to mind when feeling anxious.

When social anxiety starts to change, then meanings change also. As confidence grows, then a setback or disappointment (such as someone being unable to come with you to the cinema) no longer has its original meaning, for example about being rejected, and about not being acceptable to others. Instead of being stuck in seeing the refusal as a personal rejection, it becomes possible to step outside this framework, and to start thinking differently: trying out new 'meanings', such as 'Maybe they were busy', 'Perhaps I need to meet more people'.

KEY POINTS

- Thinking plays a central role in social anxiety.
- What you think affects how you feel. This is the basis for cognitive behavior therapy.
- There are many kinds of thinking (or cognition), and thoughts are not always easy to put into words.
- It is useful to distinguish three levels of cognition:
- – what you notice and pay attention to: socially anxious people notice things that fit with their fears;
- – negative automatic thoughts (NATs): these are like the stream of consciousness in one's head, or the internal conversation one is having with oneself or with others;
- – underlying assumptions and beliefs: beliefs about yourself, about other people and about the world are all likely to be relevant.
- Imagery can play an important, unrecognized part in social anxiety. Images are often fleeting, but they trigger strong feelings and reflect underlying meanings.
- As social anxiety changes, the meaning of social difficulties also changes. Once their significance is less devastating they will have a less distressing effect on you.

4

Where does social anxiety come from? What causes it?

Jim was sitting with a group of people during a break in the working day. They were talking light-heartedly about the new procedures for booking annual leave. During a brief lull in the conversation someone asked him: 'How do you think the changes will affect you?' Jim's mind went blank. He could not think of anything to say. He thought that everyone was looking at him, and the ensuing silence seemed to go on for an eternity, while he stared at the floor. Finally he managed to mumble, 'I don't really know,' and the conversation continued around him while he felt mortified: stupid, embarrassed, and angry with himself for not being able to answer such a simple question more easily. He was sure that he had just confirmed their general impression of him as totally inadequate.

What was the cause of Jim's anxiety? The first answer to this question is: 'other people'. Someone asked Jim a question, all the people in the group were looking at him as he tried to answer it, and for Jim other people are the cause of his problem. The question he was asked made his mind go blank, and triggered a set of events that he found acutely embarrassing, so that he ended up feeling stupid and angry with himself as well as anxious, and found the whole event undermining and humiliating. If no one had asked him a question it would never have happened.

BOX 4.1: CAUSES OF SOCIAL ANXIETY: SOME CONTRIBUTORY FACTORS

Biological factors: what you are born with, e.g.:
- an arousal system that responds quickly, is easily triggered into intense reactions
- temperament: being more or less sociable, extrovert, shy

Environmental factors: what happens to you, e.g.:
- relationships with parents and with the people who cared for you in childhood
- your experience of being evaluated, criticized, praised, appreciated, etc.
- opportunities for social learning, making friendships, intimacy, etc.
- the ways in which you learned to cope, e.g. by facing up to things or by avoiding them

Bad and traumatic experiences, e.g.:
- being bullied, victimized, left out, teased or tormented; being rejected
- having to cope without sufficient support, e.g. if parents were ill or absent, or died

Difficulties coping with demands of different life stages, e.g.:
- childhood: learning to interact with other people; stages of shyness
- adolescence: defining an identity, becoming independent, discovering sexuality
- maturity: balancing self-reliance and dependence, control and submission; belonging
- retirement: loss of the working role, or of colleagues

Stresses that affect relationships with others, e.g.:
- major moves: new home; friends or family moving away
- important changes: a first baby; having to work in a group; managing others
- competition: thinking that if you are not a winner, then you must be a loser

Other people are not the cause of the problem. The things they do can trigger the symptoms.

There is obviously more to the problem than this, but the point to be made by thinking in this way is an important one: the immediate cause of the problem is only one of many contributory factors. Causes are always complex – which is why it is difficult to answer the question 'Why?' about a particular instance of social anxiety, or the question 'Why me?' about a particular person with social anxiety. There are many factors that contribute to the problem, and they do this in different ways. Different things will be important for different people: the main ones are shown in Box 4.1.

Biological factors: what you are born wth

We all have an apparently biological disposition to feel nervous or threatened by eyes. People with social anxiety often avoid making eye contact without realizing that, for everyone, looking someone in the eye releases nervous energy. It stimulates arousal, which makes it hard to hold eye contact for long without blinking or looking away. Being stared at makes most people feel uncomfortable (so that they feel 'stared down', and then look away), and it can also be threatening to animals. Staring at an aggressive animal can hold the attacker at bay. The eye spots on the wings of a butterfly, flashed at the right moment, can put potential predators off their stride (or strike).

There are some biological predispositions that we have in common, and some that are more variable among individuals. Two of the biological sources of variation that can play a part in the development of social anxiety are to be found in the arousal system and in personality (or temperament), and these are described next.

The arousal system

First, people vary in the speed and intensity with which their nervous system responds when it is stimulated, so that they can be described as being more or less reactive. Someone with a highly reactive arousal system will respond faster, so will be likely to notice physiological changes such as an increase in their heart rate, or in the amount that they sweat, sooner and more intensely than someone whose system is less reactive.

How one describes and understands this difference between people (in cognitive terms, the *meaning* that one gives to it) is important, as it is not necessarily a bad thing to be highly reactive. It can be understood as a kind of sensitivity, and an asset to be used both in personal and in social situations; or it can be understood as a tendency to *over*-react and a sign of being *hyper*-sensitive. Intense levels of arousal and of anxiety are uncomfortable for everyone; everyone can have them, and people adapt to the system they are born with. We know that anxiety can run in families, and this suggests that there is a genetic component to a problem such as social anxiety. However, this supposed 'vulnerability factor' is non-specific, which means that people with anxious parents are statistically more likely than others to suffer from anxiety, but the kind of anxiety that troubles them may be different from the one that troubled either of their parents.

Temperament or personality

Secondly, people vary in their temperament or personality. Newborn babies are strikingly different right from the start – even if only their parents know it. Some are calm and others more excitable; some seem sociable and others less so. As they develop, some remain happier than others when on their own, and ready to entertain themselves, while others appear to prefer company. All babies are relatively indifferent to strangers at first, and they are not distressed by being handed round from person to person. Later they go through a stage of being shy and more wary of being with people they do not already know, and easily become distressed if separated from familiar people. But the degree to which strangers upset them is enormously variable.

Of course, biological differences between people are not the only factor determining how a child responds to new people, even in the first year of life. Babies are constantly learning from and responding to the reactions of those around them. So they could pick up signs of anxiety from their parents, or their parents may not be able to comfort and reassure them when they are distressed, or the strangers they meet may be insensitive to the needs of small babies and do alarming things. Nevertheless, temperamental differences between babies exist, and they may help to create the conditions in which social anxiety can subsequently develop.

Biological differences are unlikely to be the whole cause of the problem, and their effects can be modified by what happens later. Having a sensitive arousal system, or a less outgoing temperament, does not necessarily lead to social anxiety, just as being born with relatively long legs and an athletic disposition might not make someone into a good runner. It might do so, but there will be many people with long legs and an athletic disposition who are not particularly good at – or interested in – running. Similarly, there are many supersensitive people with unsociable (or introverted) personalities who are not socially anxious.

Socially anxious people often think that things would be different if only they were different in some way: better-looking, thinner, more intelligent or funnier, more interesting or sexually attractive, more creative or imaginative. The assumption behind such wishes is often that they are handicapped by being born the way they are; that there is nothing they can do to change it. The facts of the case prove otherwise. People of all kinds, whatever their assets or apparent deficits, can make friends, find partners, enjoy relationships with others and feel socially confident. Even more surprisingly to some, highly attractive, good-looking, intelligent and successful people can suffer from debilitating degrees of social anxiety. Other factors, including environmental ones, also contribute to causing the problem.

The environment: what happens to you

Social relationships are first made at home, and this goes for relationships with people in the family as well as with people outside it. In their families people learn important social lessons: about what is acceptable or not acceptable in terms of behavior; about what it means to feel loved and to feel unloved; about being accepted for what you are, or being rejected. These things happen to all of us occasionally as we grow up, and our experience of them provides the background to our beliefs and assumptions about what other people think of us. Being liked, loved and accepted by others, friends as well as family, conveys a sense of one's own personal value and self-worth, and provides the setting and conditions for building self-esteem and for feeling confident in relation to other people.

The message you carry away

The story is not a simple one, because everyone as they are growing up does some things that other people object to (tells lies, says cruel or unkind things to others, sets out to hurt somebody else), and no parent, teacher or other adult is ever perfectly fair, and always attuned to the needs of a particular child. So everyone gets it wrong much of the time; but family life does not have to be perfect for people to feel socially confident. If the overall message a person grows up with helps them to feel that they are accepted and 'belong', if it helps them to relate to others in ways that they wish to, some mishaps need not matter and do not cause problems.

If the overall message is not positive or helpful – if it is definitely negative, or if it leaves room for doubt – then some people become uncertain about their ability to relate to others, about their acceptability or adequacy or lovability, and about the ways in which people will react to them; and anxiety is built upon uncertainty. If you never know whether you will be praised or criticized, when you will get yelled at, or told to get lost, and there is no one more consistent to turn to for support, then it is harder to become socially confident. Such experiences may produce deep-seated problems, or they may cause few or only temporary difficulties, for example if it happens at home but not at school, or in one class but not in the next one. Having one staunch supporter, or one person who understands, can make all the difference.

Socially anxious people, as we have already seen, tend to think that other people pass judgment on them. They assume that they are being evaluated and that the product of the evaluation reveals that they have failed to come up to the mark. People are not born with such ideas ready in their heads, and our best guess as to where they come from is that they are a product of what happens later. The ways in which we are evaluated as we grow up, for better and for worse, tell us about what is thought to be acceptable in the social world to which we belong, and about what is not. They can help us to behave in socially acceptable ways, and help us to build the confidence that mistakes can be put right, that rejection when it happens is only partial and temporary; or they can undermine this confidence. If judgments were too harsh, too all-encompassing or too unremitting, or if they were applied indiscriminately, regardless of what actually happened, then people feel rejected, inadequate or unacceptable, and they come to fear that their actions will reveal underlying weaknesses, or fundamental sources of badness, even if no such things exist. Then they may fear doing anything that could reveal their perceived inadequacy or inferiority to others. Joining in a conversation may be sufficient to trigger such a sense of vulnerability, if it has been an important, dominant part of early experience.

The meaning of the messages

The core beliefs and assumptions listed in Chapter 3 (page 51) can be understood as an overall summary of some of the more distressing messages – or meanings – that people with social anxiety have ended up with as adults, and it is possible that these messages were derived from childhood experiences. People learn from experience such things as 'You've got to do things right to be acceptable', or 'I'm different from others, and odd'. The bad news about these messages is that they can be deeply ingrained, so that they 'go without saying', as when someone just 'knows' they are not as good as others and never even questions this assumption. But the good news is that the messages can be updated. They have been learned during experience, and they are more likely to be products of the ways in which people were treated than of any real inadequacies or fundamental unacceptability. They are messages that can be unlearned when learning how to overcome social anxiety.

When writing (or thinking) about a problem like social anxiety, it is easy to focus on problematic things, and on the factors that contribute to causing the problem, and to forget about the positive things, as if they were not relevant. However, when thinking about the messages that people pick up during their early experience, it is important to think about the more negative messages in the context of positive ones as well, and to keep the overall picture in perspective.

Everyone learns positive as well as negative things about themselves as they grow up, for example about their sensitivity, or humour, or kindness, or wish to be friendly; and one of the difficulties is that when the negative ones cause problems they tend to dominate. Positive characteristics and positive messages that other people gave us as children can easily be discounted and denied, when things go wrong, or when feeling bad. But discounting them is more likely to be an effect of feeling anxious and bad about oneself than a true reflection of the real state of affairs.

The need for appropriate opportunities

Social worlds differ enormously from place to place, and the ways in which our parents talked to their friends and to each other are vastly different from the ways we now use and feel comfortable with, and that goes for talking about ordinary things like making an arrangement to do something together, as well as for talking about things that we know people now think quite differently about, such as personal feelings or sex. All of the little niceties about how it is done have to be learned, and none of them can be learned without real-life experience. I have not been to a disco for years, and no longer know how to behave in one. I have been to a number of formal dinners, and feel confident enough to work out pretty quickly what will be required of me at the next one. I am not bothered by the possibility of putting a foot wrong in that situation, and can ask if I am uncertain about something.

Not having the opportunity to learn how things are done can put people at a disadvantage, and that goes for having the opportunity to mix with people one's own age, to find and make friends with kindred spirits, to be listened to, to confide and learn to talk about oneself, and to discover what makes other people tick. So lack of the relevant experience can also contribute to social anxiety; and gathering relevant experience can help to solve the problem. For a young person who wants to meet people, learning about discos could be much more useful – and much more fun – than learning how to handle formal dinners. But it cannot be done without going and learning what to do.

In some situations the rules of the game, so to speak, are clearer than in others. So there are standard, conventional ways of ordering a meal in a restaurant, introducing one person to another, conducting a business meeting, chairing a committee, making requests or saying 'no' to unreasonable requests. In many languages there are different forms of speech for talking to people, which vary according to how well you know them or how formal you want to be. In all of these cases, the only way to 'do it right' is to learn the rules, and it can be comforting to feel that there is a rule book to turn to in case of difficulty. But the problem is that, mostly, there is no rule book. There is nowhere one can look all the rules up; and even if there were, no one learns them all at once. So adults cannot usually approach unfamiliar situations with a complete set of social rules, ready to draw on whenever needed. They have to learn new rules for the new situations they find themselves in as they do different and new things, and learning the rules usually involves a process of approximation, whether you are joining the retirement club or negotiating with the bank manager. Sometimes you get it right, and sometimes you get it wrong. You can watch other people to see what they do, and you can ask, but when it comes to trying it out for yourself you are bound to stumble at first, and produce a more awkward and less polished performance to begin with than you will later on. The danger is to suppose that, when your experience has failed to supply you with opportunities to learn the rules, this must continue to put you at a disadvantage, socially. We know that socially anxious people do as well as others in social situations when they are not anxious. The problem is not in their basic social abilities so much as in the fact that being anxious makes it hard to take full advantage of these abilities.

Learning from the experience of problems

Another environmental factor that contributes to the development of social anxiety is to be found in the way people have learned to cope with the problems they encounter and to deal with feeling anxious. This is something that all of us learn, partly through practice and partly by watching the people around us and using them as models. We know that facing problems works better in the long run than avoiding them – or drowning one's sorrows in drink. So people who learn to hang in there, not to be too dismayed when things do not go their way and not to blame themselves excessively for the awkwardnesses that sometimes arise give themselves a better chance of learning how to cope when they feel anxious than people who, for example, focus instead on how to escape or avoid the situation, or on how to ensure that their vulnerabilities are well hidden from view. Wanting to avoid or keep safe are states of mind that perpetuate the problem, as they contain the hidden message that doing otherwise would be dangerous or risky.

Bad or traumatic experiences

Traumatic experiences cause extreme distress at the time that they occur, and they also leave their mark. They are hard to get over. Some of the most common ones reported by socially anxious people are experiences that happened at school. Being bullied is obviously one of these (the effects of being bullied are discussed in detail in Chapter 13), but they also include other ways of being singled out or made to feel different and unacceptable, such as being teased for a characteristic that one could do nothing about, like having freckles or big ears or acne, or for being overweight. When persistent, or prolonged, this kind of treatment can feel to the recipient like being on the receiving end of frank victimization or downright cruelty. The message received is a painful one that usually fits into the category of 'we don't want you', or 'you don't belong'. Surprisingly, perhaps, being singled out seems to be part of the problem, as it can sometimes have a bad effect even when it happens for supposedly positive reasons. For example, being praised at home or at school can make you liable to be picked on by those who are not, or it can make you feel like a misfit and different from others.

Being rejected for oneself is always a deeply distressing experience, and there is little doubt that it can lead to social anxiety. However, not all people who have been rejected or suffered through bad experiences become socially anxious. The reasons for this are not entirely clear, though the fact that there are so many contributory causes of the problem must be one of them. Having a bad experience is only one of many things that happen to someone, and only one of many possible things that could make that person socially anxious. When such things happen, the person to whom they happened may have been helped in a way that 'made the difference'. They may have been rescued by particular supporters, family members or friendships; or they may have developed their own interests, skills or talents, which helped them to build their self-confidence and to keep their self-respect in difficult circumstances.

Anything that singles someone out as different, unacceptable, odd or weird in the judgment of others (whose judgments may be completely wrong, of course) can make a person susceptible to social anxiety. If people have had to assume responsibilities beyond their years because their parents or the people caring for them were absent or had their own difficulties to deal with, they may have been too tired, worried or busy to have been able to take part in the social life going on around them. They may have had to grow up so quickly in some ways that they became out of touch with people their own age, and their real contemporaries may have seemed somewhat childish. It is difficult to play, to relax or to talk freely about the things that are happening to you when you are extremely distressed, worried or over burdened as a child. So the experience sets people apart at the time, and crossing the gap later can be difficult and create anxieties.

The demands of different life stages

Most people with social anxiety report that it began for them in one of two ways. Either they say they have always had it, that they have been nervous when meeting new people all their lives, and they may describe themselves as being different, odd or inherently shy people; or they say that it became a problem in their teens and early twenties. Adolescents and young people have to find their way around a large number of potential social stumbling blocks as they become increasingly independent of their families, seek out partners with whom to share their lives, and establish themselves in the adult roles that our society expects. Negotiating all of these changes successfully is no easy task, and difficulties that may have lain dormant earlier in life may make themselves all too apparent when things do not go right: when the person you find most attractive opts for someone else, when you move to a new place and your reticence makes it hard to make new friends, or when the only way you have learned to assert yourself is by being aggressive.

Patterns developed earlier may make some later problems harder to deal with. People who have always depended on having a crowd around them, at home, at school and at work, are especially susceptible to feeling isolated (and rejected) when their children leave home, or when their work requires them to move to a new place, or when they retire and lose contact with colleagues. This can undermine their social confidence, and make it (temporarily at least) hard for them to become established in a new social context.

Each stage of life presents its own set of social challenges, as can be seen from Box 4.1, page 60, and so a bout of social anxiety can arise at any stage in life.

Present stresses

Two kinds of stresses are especially likely to contribute to feeling anxious, and for people whose fears focus on their sense of what other people think about them, the anxiety is likely to take a social form. These two stresses can be summarized as major moves which sever important social contacts with friends, family or colleagues, and important changes that affect ways of relating to other people.

These events are stressful because they demand adaptation, and that takes energy at a time when there may be little to spare, and when confidence has yet to be built up. Then old vulnerabilities may re-emerge. Someone who has just been promoted may have to respond to many new demands, but may also have to start giving orders to people who were only recently friends on an equal footing; and they may have to present progress reports and future plans at meetings with 'important' people, whose judgments and criticisms may be made publicly. Working women who have just had their first baby often go through a stage of feeling unconfident – about many things – and when they are also stressed and relatively isolated, it is easy to find it additionally stressful to meet new and apparently more confident people. For them, the re-entry into the workplace later on can also bring on a similar, unconfident phase.

How do all these factors interact?

When a problem has many potential causes it is hard to disentangle them. The way in which we currently understand what is going on in social anxiety will be described in some detail in the next chapter; one relatively simple way of thinking about causes is shown in Figure 4.1. This divides the main contributory causes into *vulnerability factors* on the one hand and *stresses* on the other.

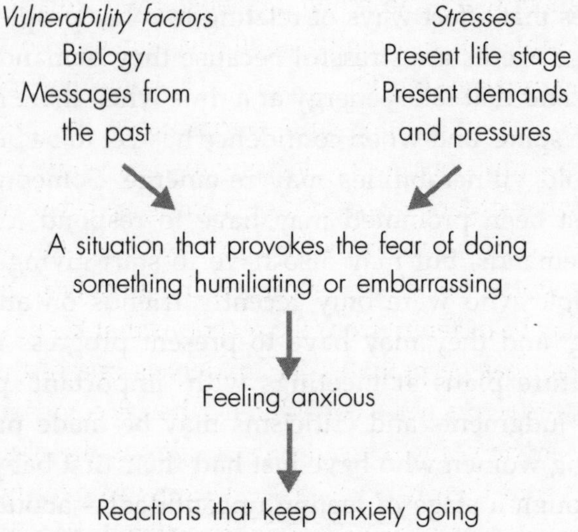

Vulnerability factors	*Stresses*
Biology	Present life stage
Messages from	Present demands
the past	and pressures

A situation that provokes the fear of doing
something humiliating or embarrassing

Feeling anxious

Reactions that keep anxiety going

Figure 4.1 Summarizing the causes of social anxiety

Vulnerability factors are long-standing characteristics that make someone susceptible to bouts of social anxiety, and they are both biological and psychological. Psychological vulnerability factors can be summarized as the messages that have been gleaned from the things that happened earlier in life – from experience. Stresses include the demands of a person's particular stage of life and any specific stressful factors or circumstances that are affecting them at the present time. These may be internal pressures, such as the desire to succeed, the need to be liked, or the fear of being alone, as well as external ones, so what counts as a stress varies from person to person.

The diagram shows that for people with social anxiety, the problem will occur when they encounter situations that provoke the fear of doing something that will be humiliating or embarrassing. Once they feel anxious then a vicious cycle comes into play, and perpetuates the problem. Reactions to anxiety, such as looking for a way out, worrying about what others might notice, feeling self-conscious or finding it difficult to speak fluently, feed back to make the anxiety worse. So whatever caused the anxiety in the first place may be different from the reactions that keep it going. The cycle that perpetuates the anxiety is one of the most important factors to be considered when it comes to overcoming anxiety. Breaking the cycle allows the anxiety to subside, and then it is easier to see how to deal with the stresses and personal vulnerabilities that may otherwise bring it back again.

Some concluding comments

People depend on each other; they always have. In primitive times, for example, being excluded from the group could have threatened a person's chances of survival. So the need to make oneself acceptable is likely to be deeply ingrained – and the ability to do so could even increase the chances of successfully reproducing and raising a new generation of children. People need a social life, for protection and for division of labour as well as for procreation. Being alone and isolated, without companions, is threatening, and hard to tolerate for long. It makes us feel vulnerable, so it is no wonder that isolation is used as a form of punishment, or that hostility and rejection are alarming experiences to deal with. It takes a huge amount of discipline and self-denial to live as a hermit, partly because having social support available provides a degree of protection. When bad things happen, those people who have support from others around them fare better than those who do not – which is not to say that social life does not have its own difficulties and dangers too.

These difficulties and dangers were all too apparent to Jim, whose inability to answer the question he was asked introduced this chapter (see page 59). He became tongue-tied and anxious when asked how the new arrangements for taking holidays from work were going to affect him. If other people were not the cause of the problem for Jim, then what was? We know nothing about the vulnerability factors in Jim's case, nor about any stresses, demands or pressures on him that there may have been. All that we know is the reflection of these things in his mind (or the 'surface' problem), and this is a common state of affairs. The surface problem dominates Jim's experience, leaving him as well as us asking the question 'Why?' First his mind went blank, as he could not think of anything to say. Then he thought that everyone was looking at him, and became aware of the interminable silence that followed. After speaking he was so preoccupied with his feelings – mortified, embarrassed, angry – that he could no longer follow the conversation, and he ended up berating himself, certain in his mind that he had, yet again, made a bad impression, and that everyone there thought of him as inadequate. The way Jim's mind works when he is anxious provides the clues for understanding what to do about the problem, and it is immediately clear that we do not have to know everything about all the factors that could have caused it in this case in order to think about how to reduce his anxiety. Jim's thoughts are central, and they reflect the many processes that are set in motion when someone else's actions trigger his symptoms of anxiety.

KEY POINTS

- Other people are not the main cause of social anxiety. Many other factors contribute to it.
- These include both biological factors and environmental ones.
- Experience of relationships as we grow up provides the framework for our thinking about how we relate to others, and bad experiences can leave long-lasting impressions.
- Social life presents different demands at different stages.
- Vulnerability factors and stresses combine to make someone susceptible to social anxiety, and a vicious cycle operates to keep the anxiety going.
- It is not necessary to know everything about what caused the problem in order to work out what to do to alleviate it.

5

Explaining social anxiety: Understanding what happens when someone is socially anxious

In 1995 two clinical psychologists who are researchers as well as clinicians, David Clark and Adrian Wells, published a new model of social anxiety. This model helps us to understand what happens when someone suffering from social anxiety encounters one of the situations that makes them feel anxious. It explains the vicious cycles that keep the problem going and it also suggests how social anxiety can be treated. Many of the suggestions about how to solve the problem in Part Two of this book are based on this model.

Of course, other people before Clark and Wells have had many ideas about how to understand social anxiety, and not everyone working in the field will explain the problem in exactly the same way, even now. However, this new model has many advantages: it is being backed up by careful research that so far has corroborated the ideas behind it; it is consistent with some of the earlier models but more specific than them, and therefore explains more clearly what should be done to overcome the problem; and it recognizes the central part played by thinking, or cognition, in social anxiety. The model can, and no doubt will, be modified as more research is done and more information becomes available.

These are important points, because it is a mistake to assume in any scientific field that theories are fixed. This means that there is no one who has the one and only right and complete answer. The model will stand or fall according to how useful it is – and this one is proving to be exceptionally useful. The assumption behind it is that social anxiety can be understood and explained. It is not a mysterious entity that will always be confusing and puzzling, and the way in which we understand it plays an essential part in understanding what to do about it. Another assumption is that models like this one, that are based on research by experienced clinicians and have been developed out of earlier models and theories, are highly likely to have got much of the story right. There will be enough truth in them for everyone who suffers from the problem to gain something from learning about them. If this particular model does not fit, or fits only partially, then it may be less useful than it otherwise would be, and it may be better to explore other ways of understanding the problem as well, and to search for other suggestions for overcoming it. But there is also highly likely to be a great deal to be gained from thinking about the ways in which this way of understanding the problem makes sense of particular difficulties, as it is a highly versatile model and provides a good way of making sense in most cases.

The current cognitive model of social anxiety

A diagram of the model is provided in Figure 5.1, and the diagram is explained here first before detailed examples are given of how it works out in practice. Although it is rather complicated, it is worth looking at the diagram and seeing how the different parts of it link together to keep social anxiety going.

We already know that the type of situation that triggers a bout of social anxiety varies from person to person. Starting at the top, the diagram shows that when one of these situations occurs it activates particular beliefs and assumptions, for example that other people are being critical or making negative social judgments. As a consequence, the situation is perceived as threatening and interpreted as socially dangerous, giving rise to thoughts such as 'I'm going to do something wrong here', 'I can't come over well, in the way that other people can' – thoughts that provoke distress and anxiety. These patterns of thinking are, therefore, at the hub of the whole process.

When this happens, socially anxious people focus in on themselves. They become increasingly self-aware or self-conscious (the central circle in the diagram). As they shift their attention inwards, onto the signs of social anxiety and social ineptitude of which they are painfully aware, and which they think that other people notice, this makes them increasingly conscious of themselves and of the way in which they think they are coming over to others. In technical terms this is described as *processing themselves as social objects*, almost as if they were able to see themselves from the outside, as an observer would.

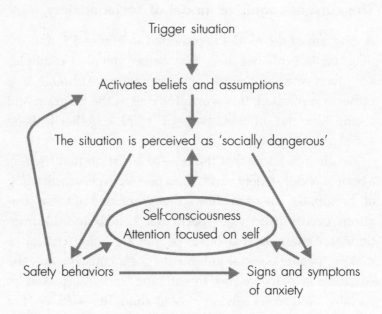

Figure 5.1   The Clark and Wells model of social anxiety

Of course they cannot actually do this, but that is how it seems to them in their mind's eye. As mentioned in Chapter 3, many socially anxious people have images of themselves when they feel anxious that fit with how they think – or fear – other people see them. They describe images of themselves doing things that to them are 'unacceptable', like blushing or trembling or stuttering, and describe their view of themselves in these images from 'outside in', as if they were able to see themselves as someone else would.

The more people focus on their own internal sensations and perceived shortcomings, the more self-conscious they become, and the more threatening, dangerous or risky the situations seem; so the arrows between the self-aware-ness circle in the centre of Figure 5.1 and the perceived social danger above it go in both directions. Focusing inwards makes people more aware of internal signs and sensations of social anxiety, and being aware of these experiences makes the situations seem more socially threatening.

It is worth noting at this point that all three levels of cognition are already present in this account of the central part of the model. The *self-awareness* cycle reflects what socially anxious people notice and pay attention to, for example the sense that everyone is looking at them; *nega-tive automatic thoughts* are involved in perceiving and inter-preting social situations as threatening or dangerous, for example 'I'm not going to be able to think of anything to say'; and *underlying beliefs and assumptions* are activated by the particular situations in question, for example 'I'm different. I don't really belong'. These three types of thinking are central to the model as well as being central to the problem of social anxiety.

Two other consequences of perceiving a situation as socially dangerous – safety behaviors, and signs and symp-toms of anxiety – are shown in the bottom corners of the diagram. It is only natural to keep yourself safe when you feel anxious or frightened, for example by talking only to 'safe' people, or about 'safe' topics; by hiding your 'real' self, or by not making eye contact. There are many ways of keeping safe. But whether or not they succeed, they lead to the conclusion that without them things might have been even worse. For example, you might think that if you had not kept a tight hold on yourself everyone would have seen your shaking, and thought the worse of you for it; or if you had spoken up and said what you felt instead of keeping quiet, you might have revealed some unaccept-able things about yourself and turned people away from you. Feeling at risk makes you want to keep safe, but trying to keep safe keeps you thinking that the situation is risky. One thing feeds into another to keep the problem going. Safety behaviors were described in more detail in Chapter 1, and a list of common ones is shown in Box 1.3 (page 13).

The diagram shows that there are three ways in which using safety behaviors can help to create vicious cycles. The arrow leading towards the top of the diagram shows how using safety behaviors means that the same types of situ-ations will continue to trigger the problem. They confirm underlying assumptions as well as reinforcing the impres-sion that you have got to keep safe, or something bad might happen. If you always take action to keep yourself safe, including when that is not necessary, this teaches you to go on taking protective action, and prevents you learning that the situations from which you are trying to protect yourself are harmless, and that the actions serve no useful function. In fact, trying to keep safe is as pointless as hanging up the garlic to keep the vampires at bay and then supposing that the absence of vampires demonstrates the value of the garlic.

The second counter-productive aspect of safety behaviors is that they focus attention inwards, and make people increasingly self-aware and self-conscious (see the arrow in the diagram from safety behaviors to the central circle). This too makes the situation seem even more threatening. Avoiding eye contact by keeping your eyes turned down (a safety behavior) makes you aware of what is going on inside and prevents you finding out more about what is going on around you. So you cannot tell when it is safe to look up again, and the situation continues to feel dangerous. Safety behaviors such as failing to look directly at people also tend to attract attention, and becoming aware of this increases self-consciousness further, so they inadvertently make the situation worse.

The third way in which safety behaviors link up with other reactions is that they can increase the signs and symptoms of anxiety rather than reduce them, as is shown by the line drawn along the bottom of the diagram. They can increase levels of tension, nervousness, shakiness or embarrassment. For example, tensing yourself up and trying to hold yourself steady makes you shake more, not less, and trying to make sure that you are not being boring makes it harder, not easier, to think of anything interesting to say. It makes you more tense and nervous and less able to come across naturally.

How do the signs and symptoms of anxiety, for example the bodily changes such as heart thumping, sweating and trembling, and the feelings of nervousness, fit in? The model shows that when a social situation is seen as threatening or dangerous, this produces signs and symptoms of anxiety such as shaky hands, which increase self-consciousness as others might notice the shaking. Then the situation seems even more threatening or dangerous. If others will notice the shaking they might judge you on the basis of this 'weakness'. It is interesting that these symptoms are often the things that socially anxious people notice most, and the things that they mention first when talking about their difficulties, but they are in some ways the last piece of the puzzle to be put into place when describing the model. This is not because clinical psychologists, and other therapists also, think that they are unimportant, but because we know that they start to subside when the things that keep them going change.

One reason why this model is useful in overcoming social anxiety is because it helps to distinguish three things that keep social anxiety going: patterns of thinking, safety behaviors and self-consciousness. Another is that it explains why the problem has not disappeared despite all the situations people have been in that have turned out to be less bad than they feared. First, becoming socially anxious focuses attention inwards, onto their inner experience – onto their own thoughts and sensations – and leaves less attention over for finding out what is really going on. Socially anxious people thus end up with one-sided or biased view of the situations that trouble them. They know all about how it feels from their own perspective and relatively little about how it seems from the perspective of others. Secondly, efforts to keep safe, even when they are not entirely successful, leave people feeling that things would have been worse if they had not tried to protect themselves, or that they have only narrowly missed a 'real' disaster – as if their social life were best understood as a series of lucky escapes.

The model in the diagram explains the main processes that keep social anxiety going; the examples provided below show how the model works in practice.

Illustrating the main processes that keep social anxiety going

Nathan was the youngest child of rather elderly parents, and he had two brothers seven and ten years older than him, who teased him mercilessly throughout his childhood. He grew up with the impression that they were the 'real' family and that he was the afterthought or appendage. All his efforts to join in, to copy his brothers and to belong, failed to change their attitude towards him. However, he greatly admired his brothers, who were more successful than he was in many of the ways that mattered to him, and he assumed that 'they were right and he was wrong'. He ended up thinking of himself as 'different', and this belief became stronger after an episode of being bullied at secondary school.

The way in which the model explains Nathan's social anxiety when he is in his thirties, and is about to join a group of people who are having a drink, is illustrated in Figure 5.2.

Joining the group activates Nathan's beliefs that he does not belong, and that he is different from other people. His immediate thoughts fit with these beliefs and although he does not put them into precise words at the time, he can later on describe the sorts of things that were going through his head: 'I'm not going to be able to think of anything to say', 'I'm going to do something wrong', 'I can't come over well'.

These thoughts reflect the degree to which this situation threatens him, and set the vicious cycles in motion. They make him feel threatened, and make it hard for him to behave normally. Immediately he focuses in on himself. He becomes aware that his mind has gone blank. He notices every silence in the conversation. He cannot grasp exactly what everyone is talking about. So he tries to keep himself safe, and the main strategies he uses are avoiding looking directly at people (he feels embarrassed, and wants to hide this from them), and simultaneously making a big effort to ensure that what he says does make sense. But while his mind is preoccupied in this way it is hard for him to listen to what other people are saying, so he becomes increasingly uncertain about whether what he has just said did make sense, and as this goes on he feels progressively more inadequate and increasingly self-conscious. As soon as he joins the group he feels the tension inside him start to build. As the anxiety increases he feels hot, fearful and panicky. It becomes hard to concentrate or to 'think straight', and he has the sense that he is talking nonsense. He is also embarrassed and humiliated by his anxiety symptoms, and this makes him feel even more self-conscious.

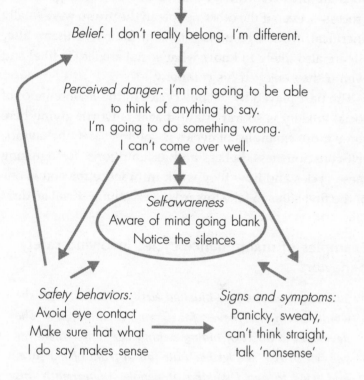

Situation: Joining some people who are having a drink.

Belief: I don't really belong. I'm different.

Perceived danger: I'm not going to be able
to think of anything to say.
I'm going to do something wrong.
I can't come over well.

Self-awareness
Aware of mind going blank
Notice the silences

Safety behaviors:
Avoid eye contact
Make sure that what
I do say makes sense

Signs and symptoms:
Panicky, sweaty,
can't think straight,
talk 'nonsense'

Figure 5.2 Practical example of the model

Regardless of whether he eventually calms down, regardless of how the situation develops, and regardless of whether anyone notices how Nathan feels inside, he will come away with the impression that situations like this one are potential sources of danger. Even though he tried to keep himself under control, and tried hard to say the right sorts of things, he ended up feeling 'different' again, convinced that others too would think that he did not really belong. His assumptions are thus confirmed by these inward-looking, cyclical processes, even if the other people in the group were totally uncritical in their responses to him (many of them, after all, are also likely to know what social anxiety is like) and even if they enjoyed his company.

The part played by vicious cycles in the maintenance of social anxiety is so important that it is worth giving here some more examples of cycles involving safety behaviors, self-consciousness, beliefs and assumptions. Recognizing these cycles and how they work in practice for you is one of the first steps to take towards overcoming social anxiety.

Examples of maintenance cycles involving safety behaviors

Sue was someone who blushed easily. The fear that she would blush was never far from her mind, and she developed a habit of hiding behind her hair. Whenever she felt at risk she let her hair fall in front of her face, and tried to avoid looking at people. Underneath this protective screen she felt she glowed like a beacon. Her mind was occupied with monitoring how red she thought she looked, and awareness of the people around her. Were they looking? Had they noticed? What were they thinking?

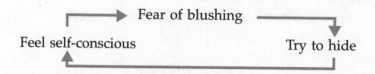

The longer it went on, the warmer, and the more distressed, she felt.

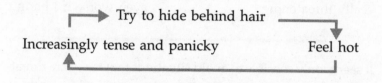

Running through Sue's head was the thought 'How can I get out of here? I need to escape.'

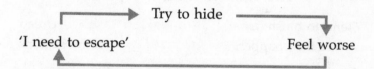

Because Sue was hiding behind her hair it was hard to attract her attention, so other people had to look closely at her to see whether or not they were getting a response.

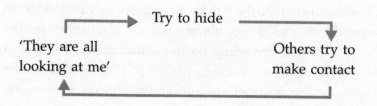

After the event, Sue thought that it might have been even worse if she had not tried to keep herself safe.

I need to keep safe –
but it doesn't entirely work

These situations are
really threatening

It could have been
even worse if I hadn't

It seems only sensible to avoid situations that really are threatening or dangerous. Sue decides in the end that the best thing for her is to keep herself safe by withdrawing a bit more.

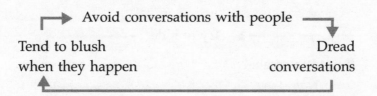

Avoid conversations with people

Tend to blush
when they happen

Dread
conversations

Of course, blushing is only one, and one of the most obvious, symptoms of social anxiety. Similar maintenance cycles are likely to be involved whenever safety behaviors are used to reduce the perceived risks of social encounters. For instance, if it feels risky to express an opinion, or to reveal personal things about yourself, then other people will at times, depending on the situation you are in and how well you know them, persist in putting you on the spot – not because they are cruel and insensitive, but because eventually they want to know more about you, and that includes knowing more about your personal likes, dislikes, activities, experiences or history. If they want to be friendly, or to get to know you, they may ask you precisely the kinds of questions that you find it difficult to answer, and they may repeat them if you fail to respond.

The cycles show that using safety behaviors, trying to keep yourself safe and to reduce the perceived risk, is an understandable thing to want to do, but it is counter-productive. Perhaps the most crucial point is that keeping safe prevents you learning that there is no need to keep safe. The situation is not really dangerous, it just seems to be so.

Examples of maintenance cycles in which self-consciousness plays a central part

Tim had always been shy. At school he kept his head down in class hoping that he would not be asked to answer questions, and it had taken him nearly 18 months to find the courage to respond to the warmth and friendliness of someone he had met at work. The relationship he now had with her was precious to him. In fact he could hardly believe his luck, and in the back of his mind he feared that at some stage, in some way, it would all go wrong. She would find someone more interesting or attractive and that would be the end of it. He was constantly worried that he was not good enough for her – that in some way he would fail to come up to the mark.

When with her, Tim became preoccupied with what he was saying: aware that he said little, and worried that what he did say might be boring.

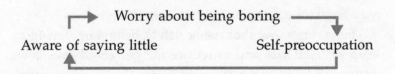

Worry about being boring → Self-preoccupation ← Aware of saying little

Focusing on himself meant that he knew more about what he felt like inside than about how he was really coming over – about what was actually happening.

Self-preoccupation (self-focus) → Fails to notice her interest ← Thinks he's being boring

He knows that he has always been shy, and that this made being a teenager into an extremely painful experience for him. The situation reminds him of bad times in the past.

Sees himself as a shy teenager (an image or a thought) → Can't think what to say ← Feels self-conscious

It is easy to see from these examples why self-awareness has been described as the engine that drives social anxiety. Being self-aware makes the situation worse because it produces the wrong kind of information. Self-preoccupation provides information about what is going on inside, which socially anxious people use as information about how they appear to others. It fills their minds with information (and images) about themselves and leaves them lacking in accurate information about how other people react to them.

Examples of maintenance cycles involving beliefs and assumptions

Rachel and Tony came from a family of self-effacing, retiring people. The family motto, had they had one, might have been 'Do not intrude'. Both of them were friendly people at heart and neither of them had had any great problems getting on with people at school. They had been ready to cooperate with others and joined in the usual array of joint activities. Being like-able people, they were able to make friends in this situation; but later on, both of them became progressively isolated and socially anxious.

Rachel's confidence was shaken when she went to college, leaving all the people she knew behind. New friends did not materialize, and she began to think that the other students did not like her or want her around.

Tony stayed near to the family home where he had found a good job, but gradually his friends moved away,

*leaving him, as he thought, the odd one out. He started
to spend a lot of time on his own, listening to music or
playing computer games, and became increasing isolated
and lonely.*

Rachel was not really shy; she just assumed that 'you
shouldn't put yourself forward', and that 'if others want
you with them, they will let you know'. So she never made
the first move, or started a conversation with someone she
did not know, or joined a group of people who were already
talking to each other. Going into the huge college canteen
became the ordeal that activated these assumptions, and
produced a situation that appears to confirm them.

Assumption: If others want you, they'll make that clear.
Thoughts: I'll be a bother to someone; I'll be in the way.
Safety behavior: Chooses to sit somewhere on her own,
out of the way.
Consequence: Other people are not sure she wants to join
in, and leave her alone. Rachel ends up thinking that
the other students don't like her: if they had done so,
they would have made it clear.

Tony was spending most weekends alone, and had done
so for many months. Then he heard that some of the people
he had known at school were getting together for a drink
in the local pub. He thought of going, and wondered why
no one had contacted him. He assumed that they would
have done so if they really wanted him to be there. By now
he knew, and supposed they did also, that he was the odd

one out. But nevertheless he felt lonely enough to want to make the effort to join in.

Assumption: If I was OK, people would keep in touch.

Thought: I'm different. I'm weird.

Safety behavior: Tony decides to go to the pub, but sits on the periphery of the group because that feels safer. However, he feel self-conscious, and worried that others will think he is odd. He finds it difficult to talk, is hesitant about saying much about himself, and he feels increasingly embarrassed as time goes on.

Consequence: People talk to each other, but not to him. Tony feels left out, odd and weird, and the less he says the less people talk to him.

The cycles involved here are quite complex, and may have many more steps in them than the simpler ones illustrated earlier. Also, Rachel's and Tony's cases show that the exact meaning of similar assumptions, and the precise effect that they have, differ from person to person. They both started with the family view that you should not intrude on other people, but ended in rather different places. No two people are exactly the same, even though the process that keeps the social anxiety going is based on the same beliefs and assumptions and has the same, cyclical form.

Examples of other kinds of maintenance cycles

The Clark and Wells model of social anxiety focuses on what happens when someone encounters one of the situations that they fear. The cycles explain why their anxiety persists in these particular situations. Similar cycles can be set in motion in other ways too: for example, before entering a situation that you expect to find socially difficult, when thinking about the situation after it is over, or when the behavior of other people appears to confirm the fears of the person who is socially anxious. Cycles of these three kinds are illustrated next.

Anticipation or dread

Many socially anxious people worry for days in advance about events like meetings or parties or encounters with people who provoke their worst symptoms, and during this time they tend to think about things that could go wrong and to dwell on possible (imaginary) disasters. The effects of anticipatory anxiety, or dread, are relatively easy to recognize. Worrying that you will shake, or say something foolish, makes you anxious, and the anxiety makes you nervous and tense ahead of time, which is enough to set the social anxiety going. Or it diverts the mind onto worrying about what other people think of you, which in turn makes any encounter with them seem even more threatening. The longer this goes on, the more likely such disasters seem, and the worse the anxiety gets. No wonder avoidance seems sometimes to be the best option – the only possible way of keeping safe from potential catastrophe.

After the event: the post mortem

When thinking about a social situation after the event is over, socially anxious people tend to engage in a kind of post mortem that confirms their own biased view of what 'really happened'. If they felt hot and flustered they assume that others noticed and judged them 'accordingly'. The symptoms that were so distressing at the time sometimes flood back again when remembering what happened – usually because of the assumptions that the socially anxious person is making. So they tend to think that other people noticed the symptoms, or thought badly about them if they did notice, or attributed the social difficulty – if indeed there was one – to them, as if they were entirely and solely responsible for how things went at the time.

As we have already seen, socially anxious people, because of their tendency to become preoccupied with themselves, often leave situations with incomplete or inaccurate information about what really went on. The post mortem is counter-productive because it can only be based on this inaccurate data. Dwelling on things after the event becomes another way of perpetuating the problem. It leads people to conclude that their assumptions were correct even though they have not really tested them out.

When awkwardness spreads

But what if being socially anxious creates real difficulties? What if the person with the social anxiety is right (or partly right) about what other people are thinking about them? Sometimes it does happen that the social awkwardness of the person who is socially anxious appears to spread to others. Someone who is anxious may inadvertently give the impression of being cold and distant, and other people may then respond to them in colder and more distancing ways than they otherwise would have done. When one side of a social interaction falters, the other may do so also. When one person cannot think of anything to say, the conversation may quickly dry up. This cycle is played out between socially anxious people and those involved with them, who may not initially be unfriendly or critical but who may appear to be so once the effects of the anxiety have become apparent.

The cause of the spreading awkwardness is not, as most people who suffer from its consequences assume, something to do with the inadequacy, weakness or unacceptability of one of the people involved. It is rather a consequence of the social anxiety, and the effects of this anxiety on the interaction. The way to overcome this problem is to learn how to break the main vicious cycles mentioned above.

The main implications for change

This model of social anxiety shows that, once the patterns of thinking involved in social anxiety are in place, the central process that keeps the problem going is a cyclical one. So the main strategy used in treatment is to break the cycles: to interrupt them, and change the patterns that keep them going. Two of the most important types of cycle are those involving self-consciousness and those involving safety behaviors. Working on these two problems, in the context of changing patterns of thinking, can sometimes be enough to solve the problem and to set in motion the processes that build confidence in a lasting way. Sometimes additional work has to be done on the longer-standing beliefs and assumptions, to find out whether they reflect an accurate or a biased view of the world, and to see whether there are alternative and more helpful perspectives that fit the facts better. Changing old habits of thinking may take longer.

KEY POINTS

- Models are useful because they explain how to understand social anxiety, and what keeps it going, and also because they suggest how to overcome it.
- The current cognitive behavioral model shows that a number of different cyclical processes are likely to play their part in keeping the problem going.
- The cycles involve all levels of cognition, or thinking: the level of self-awareness, the level of negative automatic thoughts, and the level of underlying assumptions and beliefs.
- Cycles involving self-consciousness are central to this model. Focusing attention on themselves means that people with social anxiety come away from the situations they fear with a biased view of themselves, their performance and the way that others see them.
- Cycles involving safety behaviors prevent people learning that social situations are not truly dangerous.
- Long-standing patterns of thinking that are reflected in people's assumptions and beliefs contribute to keeping the problem going because they determine the ways in which social situations are perceived and interpreted.
- Breaking into cyclical patterns of behavior that may have persisted for a long time is an excellent way of building confidence. Becoming more confident helps people to relax and to be themselves when interacting with others.

PART TWO

Overcoming Social Anxiety

Part Two of this book explains what you can do to overcome the problem of social anxiety. First some general ideas are introduced (Chapter 6); then the four main methods – changing thinking patterns, changing behaviors, reducing self-consciousness and building up confidence – are described in Chapters 7, 8, 9 and 10. Chapter 11 provides an overall summary and some ideas to help you plan what to do first. It would be best to read through these six chapters first, before starting to work on your problem, so that you can see how the ideas fit together, and then come back to the beginning and work through the suggestions more slowly.

Spend as much time as you need on each chapter, going at your own pace and applying the ideas to yourself one at a time. Some people find that their confidence grows quite quickly, and they may not need to use many of the ideas in Chapter 10, 'Building Up Confidence'. Others may find that it is not until they start to work at building up their confidence, and to chip away at things that tend to undermine it, that they make more noticeable, and steadier, progress. It is best to work up through Chapters 6 to 9 in that order so that you can build on the ideas in the earlier chapters when you come to Chapter 10.

Finally, Chapter 11 provides a summary and reminder of all the steps, and some ideas about fitting together the suggestions and dealing with some of the difficulties that arise in practice.

6

Starting points

Overcoming social anxiety involves learning how to break the vicious cycles that otherwise keep the problem going. There are four main methods:

1 *Changing thinking patterns.* This method comes first because it explains how to think again about the dangers and risks involved in social situations. Because the fear in social anxiety focuses on ideas about what other people think about you, it helps to learn how to recognize and to re-examine your patterns of thinking.

2 *Doing things differently.* Safety behaviors and avoiding things make the problem worse not better, and trying to protect yourself only makes you dread social interactions more. The answer is to face difficulties instead of avoiding them, and to take the risk of doing so without using safety behaviors for protection.

3 *Reducing self-consciousness.* This helps you to forget yourself, so that you can behave more naturally and spontaneously when with other people. The main strategies involve consciously focusing on people and things outside

yourself, and keeping more in touch with what is happening around you.

4 *Building up confidence.* Confidence may grow quickly or more slowly. When it is slow to change, this may be because you need also to work on your underlying beliefs and assumptions. You can adapt the strategies already described to help you to do this, so as to put the changes you make onto a solid foundation.

A general point

Many people who do things 'wrong' socially are not at all anxious about it. They may be awkward and abrupt, they may interrupt, or get muddled and fail to listen to what others have to say, or tell risqué jokes or interminable stories, or fall into long silences, and still people want them around and make friends with them and choose them for their partners. It may be a kind of insensitivity that allows them to be this way without being bothered by it, but it may also be mistaken to suppose that everything stands or falls according to how you behave socially. What you do may be far less important than it seems. Being yourself may be far more important, and feeling anxious certainly makes it hard to relax and to be yourself (whether you are naturally interesting, charming, tedious or repetitive). The combination of socially anxious patterns of thinking, safety behaviors, self-consciousness and lack of confidence gets in the way of being yourself, socially. These are the things that need to change.

Defining your aims

Before you start, stop and think what you want to change. You need to know what the problem is in order to start working on it, and no two people are exactly the same. So ask yourself:

- How does social anxiety affect you?
- What are the 'signs and symptoms' that bother you?
- How would you like things to be different?

Write down your answers to these questions in as much detail as you can, then turn back to Box 1.1 on page 9. There you will find some examples of the signs and symptoms of social anxiety grouped into four categories according to whether they affect your thinking, your behavior, your body, or your emotions and feelings. This list may remind you of things that you might otherwise have forgotten. It also reminds you to think about the four different ways in which the problem affects you.

You may remember that it is most unusual for someone to have no symptoms in one of the four categories shown, so if one of them is missing from your list, think again about what happens to you when you are anxious. You may, of course, be the exception to the rule, but it may also be that some of the things that happen to you have become so familiar that you have ceased to notice them. Do you avoid taking the initiative in social interactions? (This is an effect on your *behavior*; it changes what you do and how you act.) Do you make a habit of blaming yourself if something does not go 'right'? (This is an effect on your *thinking*; for example, thinking that awkwardnesses are always your fault.) Do you tend to remember the less good things that have happened to you, and that people have said about you, but forget about the better ones, and the signs of appreciation and compliments you receive? (Another effect on your *thinking*; it reflects the kinds of things that readily spring to mind, or that you easily forget.)

In order to define your aims, you need to look at the list and decide what you want to change. Be careful at this point, because it is easy to slip into being quite unrealistic. Nearly everyone sometimes feels shy or nervous, sometimes for no obvious reason and sometimes understandably: for example, before an event such as making an important announcement, or when talking to someone extremely attractive for the first time, or when broaching a delicate issue with someone in a position of authority, or when they have to make a complaint.

As some degree of social anxiety is perfectly normal, everyone has at times to deal with situations that are embarrassing or humiliating, or in which they are criticized, or judged, or evaluated less well than they would wish. Nothing you can do will stop such things happening. A useful general goal might be *to accept such events as inevitable, without letting them undermine your confidence.* The way you would behave if you reached this goal would be consistent with normal levels of social anxiety, even though it does not tell you exactly what you should try to change.

If you can be more precise than this you will find it useful later on. Precise goals help you to define exactly what you want to change – for instance, being able to look someone in the eye during a conversation, or no longer avoiding meeting new people because you feel fearful and vulnerable, or being able to ask someone in for a meal or out to see a film. Precise goals work best for two reasons. First, they provide you with specific suggestions about what to work on; and secondly, they help you define when you have reached your goal, so they also give you a measure of how you are doing. *Write down, as precisely as you can, what you want to change.* If you think it might help, look back over your list of the signs and symptoms of anxiety that you experience and ask yourself what you would like to be different. What would you be able to do, if you were anxious just in the way that everyone is? Would you feel better if you could do more things, and become involved more often with other people, in ways that you found more satisfactory, even if you still felt nervous beforehand and worried about it afterwards? Perhaps your precise goals should allow you some leeway as far as anxiety goes, as doing things in new ways, and doing new things, may well make you apprehensive at first.

Keeping track of your progress

When working on a problem like this on your own, or without help from a psychologist or counsellor or other professional, it is easy to lose track, and extremely useful to make a habit of writing things down. So, get yourself a *notebook*, or find a *loose-leaf binder* in which you can collect things together. Allocate a drawer or even a carrier bag for your social anxiety work. Without the habit of writing, and without a place to keep what you have written, you will find it hard to remember things that are important, such as how bad you were to begin with (your signs and symptoms now), what you want to change (your aims and goals), and when things went right for you as well as when they went wrong.

One reason why it is especially helpful to keep a diary or written record while you are working on your social anxiety is that many people get discouraged at first because they see no sign of change. This happens for two reasons:

- the first changes are often small;
- small changes are easily forgotten.

When you look back you tend to remember the things that went badly and forget about the things that went well, especially if these just seem to be 'normal' activities for others, like answering the doorbell, or chatting to a neighbour, or walking across a room when you know everyone can see you. One way over this problem is to use your diary to monitor your progress. You could use it for writing down what you do differently every day, or for making plans about what to do next. You could use it for doing the exercises suggested in this book, such as the ones on changing your patterns of thinking described in the next chapter. It is helpful later to be able to look back at work that you did earlier.

Trying things out and pacing yourself

Trying new things is an essential part of treatment. Overcoming social anxiety helps your confidence to grow, and deciding to do something about the problem can give you a real boost. Some of the things you try out may also be surprisingly enjoyable, but at the same time doing this work takes courage. The best strategy is to give yourself regular assignments, rather like doing homework, and to accept that you will have to take some risks – when you feel ready to do so. Doing things in a new way helps to break the old patterns, and it can feel dangerous at first – like learning to swim or to drive on the motorway in pouring rain and bad light. You will not have to do anything you consider too difficult – or anything really threatening or risky. You should also plan your homework tasks so that you can progress at your own pace. There is no rule about how fast you should go, as everyone is different.

Other people can make suggestions about what you might do, but only you can try them out. So you will need to find time for this work. If you are a very busy person you may have to decide when to give a high priority to working on your social anxiety, and decide what to give up in order to make time to for it. Just as when learning anything new, like a new language for instance, you will improve faster if you work at it little and often. Leaving large gaps when you forget about it altogether is likely to mean that you lose headway, and the gains you make may be lost again as they never had a chance to be put on a sure foundation.

Helpful and unhelpful ways of coping with the problem

Everyone who has a problem of this kind tries to deal with it in their own way, and many of the ideas they have about how to cope are imaginative, helpful and productive ones. Your own strategies may be of this kind, and you may want to keep on using them. If so, you should test them against the following principle:

Helpful strategies are those that have no long-term disadvantages.

In addition to the ones described in the following chapters, they include developing your skills, talents or hobbies, whether on your own or companionably, and learning how to relax (which is described briefly in Chapter 14) and finding ways of expressing yourself and your feelings about the predicament you find yourself in. As already mentioned in Chapter 2, this is helpful, and has beneficial effects on physical as well as psychological health, whether or not you have someone you can talk to about your difficulties, and who will listen with a sympathetic ear. Solitary ways of expressing yourself include writing about what you feel, speaking about it into a dictaphone or tape recorder, drawing pictures of how it feels, and expressing your feelings through music, or dance, or physical exercise.

Less helpful ways of coping with the problem tend to have beneficial effects in the short term, or immediately you do them, but to have harmful effects in the long term. Seeking reassurance from others is one of these. It often helps to hear someone say reassuring things such as 'don't worry', 'there's nothing seriously wrong with you', 'it will probably get better in the end', 'it's always nice to see you'. But reassurance does not last. It calms you down temporarily without solving any problems, and therefore is rather like 'getting a fix': the better it works, the more you want to seek it out next time you feel bad. Taking charge of finding your own, lasting solutions to the problem will be far more helpful in the long run.

Using alcohol to make you feel less anxious is another common, but unhelpful, way of coping, and it is easy to understand why it is tempting. Alcohol plays a part in many different kinds of social situations, and it does often have an immediate calming effect. It makes people feel less inhibited and it can make them more talkative. But as well as the obvious dangers associated with using alcohol to solve social problems, and developing the habit of using too much of it, alcohol also has a depressant effect. It is more likely to make you feel worse than better, and it interferes with sleep patterns. Many people think that they will sleep better if they have a drink or two, and indeed they do often fall asleep more quickly after drinking than they would otherwise. But they often wake during the night and then find it hard to go back to sleep again.

Planning stress-free activities: a sense of proportion

Anxiety and problems tend to dominate one's life, especially when it becomes hard not to think about them. One way of beginning to get a new perspective on the problem, and on what it means for you, is to make sure that you involve yourself in things that have nothing to do with social anxiety at all, and that you enjoy. The sorts of things that people find helpful are physical activities like exercising or gardening; recreational activities like listening to music, reading, exploring new places, watching TV, playing computer games; learning something new, like how to plaster a wall or cook Mexican food; and creative activities of all kinds: painting, drawing, writing, playing an instrument, home-making and so on. Whatever you enjoy, or used to enjoy, you should do more of. Whatever you are curious about, you should start to explore. Try to limit the effect the problem has on your life so that it does not impinge on the other possible sources of pleasure and satisfaction that are open to you.

The first approach to feeling isolated, or lonely

Being socially anxious can make people feel cut off from others. It can make it hard to build up a group of friends and to develop intimate relationships. The main aim of this book is to explain how to overcome this anxiety, and it assumes that socially anxious people want to be able to become involved with others more easily and more often, that they do not want to feel isolated and lonely. However, it is possible to recognize the value of companionship while still valuing solitary activities. It is important, and healthy, to be able to do things on one's own, and to enjoy doing them. Try to make yourself a list of solitary activities. Prompt yourself by thinking about what other people do, about things that you used to do earlier in life, or that people in your family do. If you have more solitary and lonely times than you want at the moment, try to fill at least some of them with enjoyable or interesting or challenging or creative activities that you can do – and enjoy – on your own. For example, if you enjoy seeing new places, then it would be a good idea to plan an expedition, and not to let difficulties such as having to travel and to eat on your own get in the way.

Some helpful principles to bear in mind

- Learn to recognize the vicious cycles that keep the problem going; then you can work at breaking them.
- You will need time and you will need to persist if you are to make the most of the ideas in this book, so do not worry if change comes more slowly than you would wish.
- Keep the problem in perspective. This means both keeping a check on the way you are thinking, and making sure that you do not let the problem dominate your waking life. Remember to leave time in your life for those things that you enjoy, or are interested in, and are good at.
- If you are having difficulty doing things differently, then it may be helpful to start with easy things first, and to work up to harder ones as your confidence grows.

Persistence and progress go hand in hand

The more you do, the more you will improve. Sometimes things will go well, but sometimes they will go less well, and so you may feel discouraged at times. You will be more likely to build your confidence if you can keep going despite these normal ups and downs. Everyone has good days and bad days, and problems always seem worse on a bad one. If you expect a few of these normal fluctuations they will be less likely to set you back when they happen.

Deciding how to use the suggestions in this part of the book

You have an important choice to make. You could either read through the following chapters, and use the ideas that fit for you, and that you think would work, in your own way; or you could resolve also to do the exercises described and to fill in the worksheets provided (blank copies are provided in the Appendix).

In a study of people using another, somewhat similar book we found that the people who did the exercises and filled in the worksheets gained most from their efforts. So this is probably the best strategy to adopt. But it is important to be realistic: doing these tasks is time-consuming and sometimes difficult; it can also be rather tedious, boring and repetitive. Sometimes they may even seem unnecessary. Perhaps the key point to remember is that the exercises and worksheets are examples of ways of working that other people have found useful. To be useful, they do not have to be identical to the ones provided. So you could adapt them to suit yourself, or change them from time to time if that makes the tasks more interesting, or use your notebook or diary to keep track of what you do.

Answers to some of the questions that people often ask

Should you work at becoming socially skilled?

The answer is 'yes, if you want to'; but remember that:

- *You can pick up these skills as you go.* Most people acquire their 'social skills' without being taught the 'rules of the game', just as they learn to ride a bicycle without knowing the laws of motion. You do not have to understand how it works in order to do it.
- *There is no right way of doing things.* You can be successful without being socially skilled. Many people get on well with others but are not good at these things, or find them difficult. Being socially skilled neither makes people love you nor prevents them criticizing you.
- *Skills may come naturally once you feel less anxious.* Being anxious, worried or fearful makes it hard to use your social skills.
- *Being flexible will allow you to be more spontaneous.* For social life to flow naturally it is more important to let yourself adapt as the situation demands than to practise your social skills or to learn precise rules of the game.

There are many things that people learn to do socially. Here is a list of some of them; you could probably add some more of your own:

- listening to what others have to say
- talking in such a way that others listen to what you say
- looking at others when you speak to them, and using non-verbal ways of communicating
- making conversation – in general, or to someone important like your boss, or someone you would like to go out with
- introducing people to each other
- saying no when you think it would be right to do so, or sticking up for yourself
- telling someone they have done something that makes you angry
- being aware of and sensitive to other people's feelings
- expressing your own feelings and opinions
- asking someone to do something for you; making requests

All of these skills develop with practice. A few other specific skills for which training methods have been developed, mostly for use in business or commercial settings, and which socially anxious people may also find useful, are described in Part Three, Chapter 12.

How can you learn about conventions?

Conventions are recognized ways of doing things, or patterns of behavior. Many people feel uncomfortable or unconfident if they do not know the conventions, for instance if they do not know which fork to use, or what clothes to wear. Turning up in jeans when everyone else is dressed in their best (or vice versa) can be embarrassing. This may be especially so for people with social anxiety because being the 'odd one out' attracts attention and so seems to invite judgment or evaluation by others.

There are several ways to learn about social conventions:

- *Ask*. Would you mind if someone asked you? Would it be better to admit that you do not know, or to do 'the wrong thing'? Maybe it would be polite to ask. Could you say 'I'm sorry, but I've forgotten your name'?
- *Use the information provided*. Sometimes information is there but you are too confused to take it in (e.g. notices about wearing ties, or not smoking, or laying out forks in the order they would be used in).
- *Observe*. Watch what other people do before you make a move yourself, for example before asking someone to dance. Listen to how others start a conversation, and look at the way they dress. Observe things that people take for granted, such as whether their clothes are clean and their hair washed. Look for things that tell you what is socially 'acceptable' in a

particular setting, and what is not. People in different places, interacting in different ways, develop different conventions, so there is no one right way.

Watch out for upsetting thoughts if you break a convention. In five years' time, who will remember that you sat in someone else's place or spoke out of turn at a meeting? That you had a moment when you became flushed and distressed, or that you could not hide the fact that you were bored or irritated? It is not a law of the land that you have to obey conventions. Indeed, that may be why they are called 'conventions' rather than rules or laws.

Questions about anxiety

- *Can a severe bout of anxiety do physical harm?* No. In particular, remember that increased heart rate caused by anxiety alone will not damage your heart any more than increased heart rate caused by exercise or excitement.
- *Can prolonged anxiety do you mental harm?* The symptoms of anxiety and panic by themselves, however severe, do not mean that you are developing a serious mental disorder or going insane. They are normal reactions developed to protect you in case of a real (rather than a social) emergency.
- *Does being anxious make you tired?* Yes. When you are anxious you may find it hard to cope with a normal day. Being anxious and tense is a drain on your energy. Once you have become less anxious,

you will find you have more energy for other things. This is one reason why it is important that you balance the anxiety in your life with activities that you find relaxing, enjoyable and restorative (see Chapter 14 for information about how to relax).

- *What if I am depressed as well as anxious?* Many people have periods of feeling fed up, miserable or sad if their social anxiety goes on a long time. But these feelings often lift when they start working on the problem and realize that there is something they can do about it. Depressed feelings make it harder to keep trying, but they are not a reason for giving up. If the anxiety improves the other feelings are likely to do so as well. However, *if you feel severely depressed; and if you, or people who know you, are worried about the effects that being depressed is having on you, then you should talk to your doctor about it.*

Questions about getting better

- *Should I give up trying for a while and take a good rest?* Not if having a rest becomes a way of not facing up to the problem or working out how to overcome it.
- *If I grin and bear it, will the problem go away by itself?* Possibly. Some problems of this kind do eventually diminish. But if you learn what to do to overcome the problem then you are likely to improve sooner. Also, you will be able to 'nip it in the bud' should you start to feel anxious again later.

- *Was I born this way, so that there is nothing I can do about it?* You may have been born more sensitive to stress than other people, or think of yourself as a shy sort of person, but this does not mean that you cannot learn how to overcome social anxiety and make many changes for the better in your life.
- *Should I go on searching for a 'cure'?* Nobody can cure you of anxiety altogether, as it is a normal part of everyday life. However, if you learn how to think and behave differently you will come to react to social situations differently also, and will be able to cope with them much better.

Would it be helpful to take some medication?

It could be. There are many different kinds of drugs now available for treating both anxiety and depression, and new ones are coming out all the time. Some of them are extremely effective. However, there are many issues to consider when making this decision. Although they may help you temporarily, they may not solve the problem in the long run, and some of them become less effective if you take them regularly, so that you need more to achieve the same effect. Also, if you come to rely on them, they may undermine your confidence in handling things without them. Using them regularly as a 'prop' makes it harder to build confidence in your own ability to overcome the problem, and the problem may come back again when you stop taking them. So this could be a difficult decision that it would be best to discuss with your doctor. Whatever you decide, it is worth using the ideas in this book to work at overcoming the problem yourself. In the long run, learning that you can make the changes that you want to make is most likely to help you to build the kind of confidence in yourself that helps to put the social anxiety into perspective.

If you are already taking some medication that you find helpful, then there is no need to stop taking it in order to use the ideas in this book. The two different ways of helping yourself can work together. However, if you make two changes at once, and you feel better because of them, then it is not possible to know which one helped – or whether they both did. So it is theoretically better to start one new thing at a time: either using medication or using the ideas in this book.

What if social anxiety Is only a part of the problem?

It is quite common for people who have been socially anxious for a long time to have some other difficulties as well. For example, some people suffer from periods of depression, others have difficulty being appropriately assertive, and are unnecessarily passive and accommodating, or overly hostile and aggressive, and many people have occasional panic attacks in particularly stressful situations. Many socially anxious people describe themselves as 'born worriers', and may find that at times they are beset by worries of all kinds, not just about their social lives. Most people know well that they feel less anxious after having a couple of drinks, and so it is quite common for people to start using alcohol, or various other substances, to help them feel more relaxed in company. When this becomes a habit, or the only way of coping with the loneliness or isolation that can accompany social anxiety, then one problem can easily lead to another.

If you have other difficulties as well as social anxiety, this book could still be helpful. You may have to think about which problem to tackle first, or to ask someone's advice about this, but it is still worth a try. When you decide that it is the right time to start, work carefully through it, and try not to give up even if change seems to come slowly. Remember: it is best to stick to one thing at a time when trying to make important changes in your life.

KEY POINTS

- Get yourself a notebook, or folder. Decide where to keep your social anxiety work.
- Write down your own signs and symptoms of social anxiety. Try to find at least one in each of the four categories: those that affect your thinking, your behavior, your body and your feelings or emotions.
- Define your aims as precisely as you can. Ask yourself: what do you want to be different?
- Check with yourself: how will you find the time for your social anxiety work? Can you set aside a time to think about it properly once a week? And plan to do something towards realizing your aims most days?
- Go at your own pace. No two people are the same, and it is more important to discover what works for you, and how quickly you are able to change, than to be influenced by what other people do.

7

Changing thinking patterns

Imagine you arrive at a friend's house for a meal and find the room full of people you do not know. There is a pause in the conversation as you walk in and you think: 'Everyone is looking at me.' This makes you nervous, so you leap at the offer of a drink but feel hot and conspicuous when someone asks you your name. You think: 'They must all have noticed how nervous I am', as you avoid catching anyone's eye and look round for somewhere to put your drink down in case it spills. You wonder if you will ever be able to think of anything to say and start to feel uncomfortably hot. The louder people talk the more you think 'I really don't belong here', and 'Nothing I could think of to say would interest these people'. This makes it harder for you to join in the conversation, so you keep quiet and retreat into your shell, aware of how inept you must seem in other people's eyes. You look out for a way of leaving early, hoping that you can slip away without drawing too much attention to yourself.

The next day you can't stop thinking about how you must have appeared to the other people there. Images come to mind that bring back all the embarrassment and nervousness that you felt at the time. You decide you will never do that sort of thing again. Other thoughts also go through your mind, about how hard it is to make friends, and how inadequate you feel compared to other people. You wonder if you can ever change, as you have always been shy. Other shy people seem to have managed to grow out of it, so you also ask yourself whether there is something wrong with you. The longer this train of thoughts goes on the more dispirited and the sadder you feel.

This example shows how thoughts, feelings and behavior influence each other all the time to keep social anxiety going, and it has been written to illustrate some of the many ways in which patterns of thinking can affect people who are socially anxious or shy. Read it carefully and count the number of thinking patterns you can find. Only some of them are described as thoughts, to show something of the huge variety of ways in which what is in your mind can work to keep social anxiety going: in this case, wondering, deciding, becoming aware of yourself and having images are all involved. The last paragraph shows how one thought leads on to another, in an increasingly distressing stream which reflects the meaning to you of what happened, and its implications – as you understand them.

Different kinds of thoughts

You may have noticed your thoughts, and the way that they can make you feel anxious and affect how you feel and what you do, or you may hardly have noticed them at all. When they go unnoticed this may be partly because thoughts, or cognitions, are of many different kinds, and partly because there is often no reason to express them in words. This is not something that people usually ask you to do, and making the attempt can sometimes provoke the feelings that go with the thoughts, and make you feel worse. Nobody really wants to think about exactly how foolish they appeared. Nevertheless, it is important to know about the different types of thoughts, so that you will be more likely to recognize them when you have them. They include ideas, expectations and attitudes; they may come as images, impressions or memories; they may be beliefs and assumptions or 'rules for living' that go without saying. All of these ways of thinking reflect what goes on in your mind in different ways, and they can all play a part in the vicious cycles that keep social anxiety going. This is true even if you are not fully aware of some of them, and even if you do not usually put them into words, or recognize them as 'thoughts'.

Some examples may make this clearer. Thoughts can be like half-formed ideas, for instance about being different from other people without being able to say exactly how. They may be reflected in images or impressions of yourself which come from an earlier stage of life. These could be based on memories of a particularly painful experience, such as being rejected or bullied, or singled out for criticism.

Many people, for example, report suddenly feeling small when confronted by unexpected criticism, or by someone in authority over them, and they describe having related images, such as an image of themselves as a child facing up to a large and critical teacher. Often such images have something in common with what is happening in the present, even when the person who has them cannot immediately recognize what this is.

Expectations like expecting to be judged are common in people who are socially anxious, and having an expectation is more like having an attitude that influences the way you think about things, than having a thought. Negative beliefs, for example about being inadequate or incompetent or unacceptable, often go with low self-confidence ('I can't ever seem to do things right'). Thinking this way also reveals a lack of belief in yourself. Beliefs that influence social anxiety may be about other people as well as yourself. For example, you may believe that everyone is always watching out for other people's failings and noticing their shortcomings, or that everyone is more confident and competent than you are. If this is what you believe, then you may have developed assumptions and rules for living that fit with this belief, such as 'If you do something stupid people will criticize and reject you', and 'Never stick your neck out. Make sure you keep yourself well in the background'. These are all ways of thinking, and some of them are harder to recognize than others.

The main strategies for changing thinking patterns

This chapter describes the main strategies for dealing with thoughts that make you feel bad, and that help to keep the social anxiety going. Despite the complexity of the examples above, the strategies are quite straightforward. Basically there are two steps: learning how to identify what is in your mind, what you think; and learning how to re-examine the ways you think. So even if your problem seems to be confusing, and you find it difficult to disentangle its different aspects, the straightforward examples in the rest of this chapter should help you to learn what to do, and start you moving in the right direction. This chapter focuses on thought patterns that are relatively easy to recognize, including some that are relevant to everyone – even those people who are only rarely socially anxious. Chapter 10 focuses on the types of underlying assumptions and beliefs that can make it hard to build up more confidence in yourself socially, and can therefore slow down your progress if you do not make a special effort to change them also.

In brief, the aim of the strategies described in this part of the book is to learn how to tune in to your thoughts and then to take another look at them. The idea is that the way you are thinking keeps the social anxiety going. It is what you are thinking that reveals what social situations mean to you and that explains why particular situations seem to be 'socially dangerous' – to be risky or threatening. Finding another way of seeing things will make you feel better and be more helpful to you.

Step 1: find out what you are thinking

The first step is to become aware of what runs through your mind when you feel tense or anxious. This is easier said than done because the sorts of thoughts – and images – that make anxiety worse are often difficult to identify. They come and go quickly, and may also have become automatic. They may be like bad habits: you may not be fully aware of them because they are so familiar, as if you had been looking through tinted spectacles without knowing that they were there.

Think now about a recent situation in which you felt socially anxious. When you can remember the situation quite clearly, try to answer these key questions.

Key questions for step 1: identifying your thoughts

- What went through your mind when you started to feel anxious? And after that? And when it was all over?
- What was the worst thing that might have happened at the time?
- What is it about this situation that matters to you?
- What does having this experience mean to you?
- What does it mean about you?

Did any of your thoughts make you feel worse? If so, which ones?

When identifying the thoughts that are important and relevant for you, look for those that fit with the way you felt. Sometimes it is easy to make this fit: if you felt embarrassed and remember thinking that you might have offended someone by mistake, then this obviously seems to fit. Sometimes it is much harder. For example, you might have felt totally rejected, even though nothing that you can remember seems to have provoked that feeling. When this happens, keep asking yourself the key questions. Try to stand back from the problem far enough to identify your personal perspective on it. Maybe the pervasive feeling (for example, a sense of being rejected) reflects one of your attitudes or beliefs, or particular memories that you have, and thinking about what the situation means to you and why it matters to you helps to identify these thoughts.

Using a three-column 'Thought record for identifying thoughts', like the one shown below in Table 7.1, is a good way to pinpoint thoughts, and it also helps to separate them from the feelings that went with them. A blank copy of this worksheet for you to use is provided in the Appendix (together with copies of the Key Questions and of other worksheets that will be described later). Writing things down is a good way of developing the habit of recognizing what you are thinking, and noticing how your thoughts influence the way that you feel. So make yourself some copies of the worksheet, or draw it out in your notebook, and keep a record for a few days of situations in which you feel anxious or upset. Always start by thinking of specific situations or incidents that happened to you recently, and that you remember well. Use these as cues to help put into words the things that go through your mind when you are anxious: the thoughts, ideas, attitudes, images and so on, as in the examples provided. Make yourself a copy of the key questions too, and keep it to hand, so that you can use them as prompts. Note down:

- details of the situation; what it was and when it occurred;
- what feelings you experienced (e.g. fear, anxiety, fed up, shaky);
- your thoughts, or what was in your mind when you felt that way.

Your aim at this stage should be to pay close attention to your thoughts when you feel anxious or upset. See if you can put into words the things that go through your mind, as in the examples shown in the table.

You may find this difficult if it seems to you that the anxiety just comes 'out of the blue', without there being any thoughts behind it; if so, it may be worth doing something that makes you feel anxious, just so that you can pay special attention to the thoughts that run through your mind when you do. Another option is to ask yourself the key questions about what the situation means about you, or means to you, as answers to these questions may help you put some of your attitudes and expectations into words. These are not like thoughts that run through your mind at the time, but they are still 'cognitions', and can have a significant impact on the way you feel, and on what you do when confronted by a difficult situation.

TABLE 7.1: THOUGHT RECORD FOR IDENTIFYING THOUGHTS

Situation (be specific)	Feelings (there may be more than one)	Thoughts, impressions, etc. (keep the different thoughts separate)
The boss asks to see me	Nervous Worried	He thinks my work is no good
Left alone with an attractive person	Terrified Miserable	I'm making a fool of myself Nobody likes me much
Going out with friends to the bar	Panicky Shaky Heart racing	They'll think I'm odd I can't tell jokes
An acquaintance drops in	Embarrassed	I can't relax and be normal
Remembering being stuck for words	Flustered Mortified	I'm useless I can't do things right
Thought I'd said the wrong thing	Ashamed Fearful	I'm as red as is humanly possible
A colleague got angry with me	Humiliated Rejected	Feel small and insignificant, like I did at school

It is useful to be as accurate in observing your feelings and thoughts as you can, and it is easy to forget. So use your notebook and keep it to hand as far as possible. Get into a habit of making a mental note of what happens and writing it down as soon as you can. If you always start by thinking about specific situations, about things that have happened to you quite recently, you will find it easier to identify the thoughts because you will know where in your memory to start looking for them. It is important not to just dwell on the feelings themselves, but to use them to prompt you to think about your thinking. Doing this exercise is like becoming an expert mechanic who listens to the sound of the engine, watches how the car performs, and then tunes in to possible sources of trouble.

Sometimes people feel bad – anxious, nervous or embarrassed, for example – apparently for no reason at all. However, there always *is* a reason; it just may be difficult to work out what it is. The thoughts come and go quickly, and attitudes and beliefs do not have to be put into words to influence how you feel. Think about any memories, fleeting images or general impressions that occurred when you felt anxious. This often helps in understanding why you felt so bad at the time. It may help you to recognize how your thoughts – what happens in your mind – keep the problem going. If you had an image of being yelled at in public and wanting to run away and hide, it would not be surprising to feel distressed and conspicuous. Such impressions may continue to influence the present even though they really belong in the past; and images provoke strong feelings, so they tend to keep the vicious cycle of thoughts and feelings spinning.

Patterns of biased thinking

Different kinds of thoughts typically occur before, during and after the situation that caused you problems. Before the event you may make *predictions*: predicting that you will do or say something wrong, or in some way reveal your 'inadequacy'. During the event many people go in for *mind reading*, or guessing how other people are reacting to them and what they are thinking; or they *catastrophize*, and assume that what happened was far worse than it really was. Afterwards it can be difficult to stop dwelling on what you think went wrong, judging and criticizing yourself and making assumptions about how you came across and how others reacted – like doing a *post mortem*. These are all biased ways of thinking – biased in the sense that they are influenced by the habit of taking an anxious perspective on things – and therefore they are likely to be inaccurate. Like looking through a pair of distorting spectacles, these ways of thinking are especially likely to be associated with *misperceptions* and *misinterpretations* about what is really happening, as well as with feeling bad.

Getting rid of the bias and getting your thoughts back in perspective will make you feel better, but first you need to recognize that the bias is there. Some common forms of bias are summarized below, together with some examples of the thoughts that might go with them. The reason for explaining them here is that most of us have preferences, which may help to explain why we readily fall into habitual patterns of thinking. Once you have identified your preferences, you will be in a position to spot the thinking bias in action: 'There I go again – mind reading or guessing what other people are thinking', for example. If you can do this you will have made a major step in overcoming your social anxiety.

- *Taking things personally*. Supposing that somebody else's actions were directed, personally, towards you: for example, when someone leaves the room or looks away while you are talking.
- *Taking the blame*. Taking responsibility when it is not yours: 'He was really angry. It must be my fault. I wonder what I can do to make it better?'
- *Mind reading*. Believing that you know what others are thinking: 'She thinks I'm not talkative enough'; 'He doesn't like people who are shy'; 'They know just how hopeless I am at this'.
- *Discounting the positive*. Rejecting good things as if they did not count (or using a negative filter): 'She only said that to make me feel better'; 'Anybody should be able to order a meal. Doing that OK is no big deal'; 'They were just being polite'.
- *Emotional reasoning*. Mistaking feelings for facts: 'I'm so embarrassed, I know everyone is looking at me'; supposing you *are* inadequate because that's the way you feel.
- *Catastrophizing*. Thinking that if something goes wrong it will be a disaster: 'If I put a foot wrong this relationship is totally doomed'; 'If this goes badly I will never be able to show my face here again'.

- *Over-generalizing*. Assuming that because something happened once, this means it will always happen: for example, because you spilled a drink, or failed to see a joke, you will always do something clumsy or miss the point.
- *Predicting the future, or fortune telling*. 'I'll never be able to feel comfortable talking to someone attractive'; 'I'll always be on my own'; 'Nobody will ever invite me along'.
- *Labelling, or name-calling*. 'I'm useless . . . inept . . . stupid . . . inferior'; 'Other people are unfriendly . . . critical . . . hostile . . . superior'.
- *Wishful thinking*. Supposing things would be better if they were different. 'If only I were cleverer . . . more attractive . . . wittier . . . younger . . . more like others.'

Step 2: looking for alternative ways of thinking

Looking for alternative ways of thinking is one of the main things you can do to make yourself feel better. The rest of this chapter explains how to do this using pencil and paper, and how to do it in your head. More methods are also described in the next three chapters on doing things differently, reducing self-consciousness and building up confidence. All these strategies can be used to help you to rethink your attitudes to your social life, your assumptions about it, and the way that you approach it.

Once you know what you are thinking the next step is to re-examine your thoughts. The aim is to learn to question your thoughts, rather than accept them as facts; to explore them, and the facts that spring to mind when you think about them, to see whether they fit together, make sense and are helpful to you. When you do this you will find that there is no one right way of seeing things. Rather, there are many possibilities, some of which can make you feel worse, and others of which can make you feel better. Thinking when you are having a meal with a few people that everyone else is doing things right, but you are doing them wrong is only one of the many options – and one which fits with feeling so tense and nervous about what you say and do, and so self-conscious about it, that it becomes hard to relax or to eat, or to think of anything else. Here are some of the other options:

- everyone is doing some things 'right' and some things 'wrong';
- nobody but you is thinking in terms of right and wrong anyway;
- there are so many different ways of doing things that it matters little which you choose;
- people are more interested in what you think than in whether you do things the 'right' way;
- doing things differently from others makes people curious about you, but nothing more than that.

The point is that there is a far wider choice of ways of thinking than springs to mind at first. You could see the clouds in the sky as a sign of rain, and feel disappointed, or you could see them as a chance of sunshine and feel altogether more cheerful, but there are many other options as well. The main idea is that the way you think, and what you choose to think about – given that you can learn how to choose to think about something in different ways – will affect the way you feel. Learning how to think things through gives you more control over the way you feel.

For example, someone who thought, 'They think I'm peculiar' would be likely to feel unhappy or rejected. They might feel less upset if instead they asked themselves, 'How do I know what they are thinking?', and then answered that question with the new thought, 'Maybe I'm just guessing. I may be no odder than lots of people.' Often socially anxious people are making guesses such as this one, and jumping to conclusions about what others think of them.

What would you think if someone you knew well but had not seen for a while passed close by to you in the street but did not even smile? Would you think something like, 'I must have done something to offend them', or 'I don't suppose they really like me'? If so, this is a good example of the kind of guesswork that ties in with the fear that others will think badly about you, but which is not based on the facts of what happened. Stop and think for a minute about what you would really think in this situation.

Questioning your upsetting thoughts

You can learn to find alternatives to upsetting thoughts such as those described above by asking yourself some more key questions. Here are some of the questions that other people have found useful. It might be worth copying these out into your notebook, so that you have got them to hand when you need them.

Key questions for step 2: looking for alternatives

- *What are the facts?* What evidence do you have to support what you think? What evidence is there against it? Which way of thinking fits best with the facts? The fact that you think something does not make it true.
- *What possible alternatives are there?* What would you think if you were more confident? How might someone else view this situation? What would you say to someone else who was thinking in this sort of way? What would someone who cared about you say?
- *What is the worst possible way of seeing things,* or the worst thing that could possibly happen? What is the best way of seeing things, or the best thing that could happen? Which is most realistic? Or most likely to be right?
- *What biases might be affecting your thinking?* For example, are you jumping to conclusions? Exaggerating? Over-generalizing? Are you predicting the future as a certainty? Or mind reading? Or focusing on the negative side of things at the expense of everything else?
- *What can you do that would be helpful?* What personal

skills and strengths do you have to help? What past experience of dealing with similar problems? What help, advice and support are available to you, from others or from books? What can you do to change things? If you can't change the situation, can you keep an open mind about what it means?

Answering your upsetting thoughts

Use these questions to help you to rethink, and write your answers down, so that you do not forget them. A simple two-column thought record on which to do this is shown in Table 7.2, and a blank version of this form for you to copy, together with the key questions, is provided in the Appendix. The aim is to search your mind for other ways of thinking, recognizing that these may not come easily at first. Some examples have been provided in Table 7.2, and a space has been left for you to use, if you wish, to re-examine your thoughts about being ignored by someone who knows you well. Can you find another way of thinking about it?

Sometimes people think they can re-examine their thoughts without writing things down – doing it in their heads – and, indeed, sometimes they are right. Nevertheless, for everyone it is important to do this exercise in writing enough times to be sure that you really can identify alternative ways of thinking and put them into words. Otherwise it is tempting to be satisfied with a rather vague notion of another way of seeing things, and vague ideas are less likely to have a beneficial effect on how you feel than ones that are clearer. Putting the new ideas into words, which you are forced to do if you complete a thought record like the one in Table 7.2, brings them into focus.

TABLE 7.2: THOUGHT RECORD FOR LOOKING FOR ALTERNATIVES

Upsetting thoughts (take one at a time)	Possible alternatives (there may be more than one)
I sound really stupid	Perhaps everyone does once in a while Even if I did, it would not mean I was stupid
They can see how nervous I am	Possible, but that needn't make them think I'm a bad person. Maybe they are thinking of other things altogether, and have not even noticed me
That person completely ignored me	

The essence of the method is to keep an open mind, and not to get led astray by your fears. These tend to push you into extremist positions: 'Everyone could see that I made a complete idiot of myself', rather than leading you towards a more balanced, and usually more accurate, way of seeing things, as in the examples below:

- Maybe people are not judging or evaluating me, or even noticing me particularly.
- Maybe I can't tell what people are really thinking.
- Maybe I feel worse than I look.
- Maybe people don't reject you for being nervous – after all, it happens to everyone sometimes.
- Maybe I'm just as good as they are, underneath.

Give yourself the benefit of the doubt. Try to think as you might if you had none of the bad feelings that have sent you in search of help. Take yourself on a mind-trip, and see if you can find other perspectives to explore.

Finding 'good' alternatives

Good alternatives come in many shapes and sizes, and you are the person who can judge whether the ones that you find will work for you. A good alternative is one that makes you feel better, that fits with the facts (not with your fears or suspicions, or with a biased interpretation of the facts) and that helps you to do the things that you want to do. You could look at the alternatives that you find alongside the goals that you set yourself to begin with, and ask yourself whether the new way of thinking would help you to achieve those goals.

Good alternatives also help you to break old patterns of thinking like the biases listed earlier. Watch out for your preferences and see if you can spot them in action at times when you feel bad: 'There I go, discounting the positive things again.' Unlike biased ways of thinking (especially catastrophizing, or over-generalizing), helpful alternatives can usually be phrased in moderate or 'open-minded' language, as in the 'maybe' examples listed above. They make you feel less pressurized, and help you to adopt a balanced and flexible view of things rather than an extremist one.

PRESSURIZING THOUGHTS

Examples of pressurizing thoughts would be 'I *must* think of something interesting to say', 'I *should* be able to like people more', 'I *ought* to try harder to be amusing and entertaining'. Pressurizing thoughts contain pressurizing words, like *must*, *should* and *ought*, which many people use to motivate themselves, or to urge themselves on to do better and to 'improve'. They work against you because the pressure adds to the tension and anxiety, and because they suggest that there are definite rules that you *must* obey rather than various sets of conventions which have grown up gradually and that in practice are frequently broken. Think of the people you know who break the conventions but do not worry about it.

Looking for less pressurizing alternatives may feel uncomfortable at first, as if something bad might happen if you did not do what you 'ought' to do. One way round this problem is to try thinking in terms of preferences, not pressures. Prompt yourself with: 'It would be better if . . .', rather than push yourself with 'must', 'should' or 'ought'.

EXTREMIST THOUGHTS

Extremist thoughts contain extreme words such as *always*, *never*, *totally*, *nobody* and so on. 'They *totally* ignored me', 'People *never* like me', 'I am *always* messing things up', '*Nobody* feels shy after the age of 30'. By their very nature, extremist statements are most unlikely to be true. Perhaps they could be true, but it would be worth taking notice if this happened: like being able to run a four-minute mile, or meeting someone as clever as Einstein.

Sometimes the pressurizing and the extremist words come together: 'You *should always* be polite', 'I *should never* show that I am angry', 'You *must always* let other people come first'. These statements are like rules for living, and they tie in closely with the underlying beliefs and assumptions that everyone absorbs and internalizes as they grow up. In some circumstances they make sense – and these examples illustrate well the kinds of things that parents and teachers tend to say, and the kinds of 'rules' they may try to incorporate into the home or the classroom. However, we are all at times impolite, angry and in pursuit of our own goals. We often want to do things our own way irrespective of what others want. So, instead of combining the pressure and the extremism when this happens – and hitting yourself with a 'double whammy' – it helps again to look for more balanced and moderate ways of seeing things. Instead of using phrases that sound like hidden threats – as if there were an unspoken 'or else . . .' behind them – look for more helpful alternatives. Threats work less well than rewards when you are learning something new, and they also add to feelings of nervousness, apprehension and anxiety.

Some of the options might be: 'Things often work out better if you can be polite', 'Everyone gets angry at times – but it does make a difference how you show it', or 'It's perfectly all right for me to come first at times'. Note how these more balanced alternatives point the way forwards, and define the kinds of strategies that it can be helpful to develop, such as ways of negotiating differences, expressing anger and taking turns.

What makes searching for alternatives difficult?

'YES, BUT . . .'

Being anxious goes with worrying about what might happen next; about what else could possibly go wrong, and about how bad it would be if it did. This makes it easy to doubt any new perspectives, and to follow each one up with a 'Yes, but . . .': 'Yes, I know they seemed to like me, but they don't really know what I'm like', or 'Yes, I didn't say anything stupid, but then I hardly said anything at all'. Doubting is another way of discounting, and the way to overcome it is to use the strategies of cognitive therapy: identify the discounting thought and re-examine it, to see if it really makes sense. *Maybe* people cannot tell what you are really like until they get to know you better. *Maybe* saying more, and taking more initiative when you are talking to people, would be a fairer test of your thought about appearing stupid.

Another difficulty with finding alternatives arises when people pay too much attention to the internal voice that puts them down, or deals out the criticism, or hands out the blame when things appear not to go well. All of us engage in an internal conversation with ourselves at times, as if we were talking – usually, though not always, inaudibly – to another self: 'you fool' we say – as if we did not know that quite well already. This internal monologue, or dialogue, tends to incorporate messages that we have heard elsewhere. Sometimes it has recognizable characteristics of our parents, teachers or friends: 'If you don't speak up, no wonder people can't hear what you say'; and sometimes it reflects our own self-opinion: 'You're useless.' The trouble with this internal voice is that it comes from inside, and is far more likely to reflect opinion than fact. Once again the answer is to stick to the facts, and not to be misled by some outdated ways of thinking that may have little to do with the present, and which make you feel bad.

FEELING LOW

Feeling discouraged, demoralized or depressed also makes it hard to see things another way. It is as if the black mood colours the way we see things, and places a negative filter on the way we think. If this happens to you, the first step is to remind yourself how close is the relationship between thoughts and feelings. Think about a time when you felt different, and scan your memory for specific examples of how you thought about things then. You will need to see if you can amplify the scanner, and focus it clearly, as such examples can become nearly invisible when a low mood spreads a confusing, obscuring haze over everything. The main idea to hold on to is that feeling that something is true does not make it true, although it does make it difficult to see it another way until you focus hard on the specifics of exactly what happened, and disentangle the facts from your feelings about the facts.

How to make it easier for yourself

Most people who have suffered from something as debilitating as social anxiety or shyness, something that can interfere so profoundly with their lives and with the way that they would like to be when with other people, try hard to overcome their difficulties. They do whatever they can – and often their ideas are good ones. They try to keep going, and not to run away from things. They try to 'say something to themselves to make themselves feel better' – which is a fairly good description of the general aim of cognitive therapy provided by someone who had suffered from the problem for over 15 years before seeking help for it. They try not to dwell on the problem and on the uncomfortable sensations that it produces. They try to relax and to keep things in perspective, and to build their lives as best they can. So it is not for want of trying that the problem persists. Targeting these efforts more effectively and more efficiently, so that they succeed in breaking the vicious cycles that otherwise perpetuate the problem, is highly likely to be more helpful. But it may be difficult at first. Doing new things in new ways can be alarming and feel risky. Helping yourself takes courage and it takes persistence.

If you knew someone else who was undertaking such a task, how would you set about helping them? What would they require from you? Three important contributions to their efforts would be compassion, understanding and encouragement, and it is far easier to see how to give these things to someone else than to oneself. Most people make themselves exceptions to the rule when it comes to 'self-improvement', or 'self-help', and go in for self-blame, criticism and name calling instead. 'It was all my fault', 'I'm clumsy and awkward', 'Wimp', 'Coward'. These are obvious examples of negative and unhelpful ways of thinking, and shy or anxious people can be far more creative than this when putting themselves down. It would be easier to make effective changes if you became more compassionate with yourself, and spent some time working out how to understand your own particular version of the difficulty and what keeps it going. This would be far more likely to encourage you in the effort to change. Although this may sound obvious – or trivial or patronizing – the point is worth making because it is so easy to ignore the damaging effect of saying such things to oneself.

In the next section there is a summary of the ideas in this chapter and some more ideas about how to put them together so that you can use them effectively to change the way you feel, and to help you when starting to do things differently.

Putting the steps together

The two steps for changing thinking patterns are learning how to identify what is in your mind and learning how to re-examine the ways you think. Putting these two steps together helps you to get better at finding the ways of thinking that make you feel better, and it also helps you think about how to put the new ways of thinking into effect: how to start changing your behavior as well as your thinking. Changing behavior is the topic of the next chapter, so here we will concentrate on combining the steps for changing patterns of thinking.

The way to do this is shown in Table 7.3, and blank copies of the complete thought record for you to copy and use as you wish are provided with the other blank worksheets in the Appendix. You will notice that there are two extra columns in the complete thought record that did not appear in the two earlier parts of it. The first of these, 'Change in feelings', is for noting down how working on your thoughts changed the way you felt: all of the options are available, from making you feel much worse (−10), through no change at all (0), to making you feel much better (+10). As you will see from the examples, some new ways of thinking have less effect than others, and some, like the last one shown here, may still give you some ideas about what to do even if they do not, at the time, make you feel any better. Remember, you are looking for new ways of thinking that make you feel better and that help you to do the things that you want to do, and it may take some practice before you can find them successfully.

TABLE 7.3: COMPLETE THOUGHT RECORD

Situation (be specific)	Upsetting thoughts (keep the different thoughts separate)	Possible alternatives (there may be more than one)	Change in feelings (–10–0–+10)	Action plan (what would you like to do differently?)
Talking to C. at a party. Getting stuck.	I've got nothing to contribute.	Not 'nothing', just rather little. I have, but I can't get it out.	A bit better: probably + 2 or 3	Think how to start conversations. Listen to how other people do it
	He must think I'm hopeless.	I don't know what he is thinking. There are two of us here. It could be partly him.		Move away when I get stuck, and try talking to someone else.
Picking up my drink from the table, in the pub with sports team; hands shaking.	They will notice the shaking. It gives me away.	OK, they might notice. But shaking is no big deal. Anyone might do it sometimes.	A lot better in theory. If I could really believe this I would feel + 8. In fact it's about + 6.	Try to stop bothering about the shaking, and do things anyway. Start talking to people more, instead of noticing how I feel.
	They will see through me, and discover how inadequate I am.	They seem to need me on the team, so I can't be totally inadequate.		
Dreading going to work. Hoping no one will ask what I did at the weekend.	I could call in sick.	That would only make me feel worse: and ashamed of myself.	Still dread going, but know I will feel better if I do than if I don't.	I could ask people what they did, and see if it gives me more ideas. I need to plan something, whether or not there's someone to do it with.
	I could invent something to tell them.	Yes, but it wouldn't be true – and they might catch me out.	Probably still feel just as anxious: no change = 0.	
	Everyone else but me has a busy social life.	Maybe. But maybe not too. I don't really know – yet.		

The second new column is headed 'Action plan', and asks you to think about what you would like to do differently. The point of this column is to remind you that you will gain most if you are able to put the new ways of thinking into effect to change your behavior as well as your thinking. The next chapter explains more about how to do this, and here you should think about what you would like to be able to do differently, so that you can then work towards this, by degrees if it is too difficult to do all at once. You can use any of the ideas in this book to start you thinking about what kind of action plan you would like to be able to make for yourself. The examples in the completed record shown in Table 7.3 have been constructed to illustrate how to use this worksheet, and should make the whole process clear. But remember, if you have difficulty with it, you can adapt it to suit your needs better. Many creative, socially anxious people make up their own ways of doing this work, and use their notebooks to keep their own versions of these records.

It is important to be honest with yourself when you fill in these worksheets, even if facing up to the difficulties that you have, and to thoughts that much of the time are only half realized, makes you feel worse at first – or makes you feel embarrassed. As you get better at finding alternatives, you will be able to use the method to change the way you feel, and to devise the action plan that you want.

It is also important to do this exercise on paper. Thinking things through in one's head is far more difficult than it might seem, and it is easy to skim over difficulties or to formulate rather vague alternatives and plans if they do not have to be written down. As the method becomes familiar to you, you will be able to dispense with the writing, and do more of it in your head, in the situations that actually provoke your anxiety. As one person said when she tried this, there is a risk at first of being suddenly carried away on a mounting rollercoaster of anxiety, and of getting in such a flap that you can no longer think rationally or clearly. However, what she discovered was that if she found a way of taking a break and calming down, then she could 'take stock and get a grip', and rational thought could return. This person also reminded herself that she was trying to change patterns of thinking that had been there for years – and no one had said it would be easy. It does get easier with practice, and when the methods for changing patterns of thinking described in this chapter are combined with those for changing behaviors, reducing self-consciousness and building confidence that are described in the next chapters.

Making flashcards, to help you remember new patterns of thinking

Old patterns of thinking are like bad habits, and tend to come back again and again, and it is only too easy to slip into your favourite biased ways of thinking (see pages 104–6). One way of helping yourself to break these old habits is to make flashcards that help you to develop new habits. Flashcards are small reminders of new ways of thinking that you can carry around with you. The reason why people use cards is that cards last longer than bits of paper, and they can be put in your pocket or wallet and kept to hand more easily than your notebook.

So get yourself a card, and on one side of it write one of your typical upsetting thoughts, such as 'Everyone can see how nervous I am', or 'I always make a fool of myself', or 'They think I'm not worth having around', or a question about your favourite bias: 'Am I mindreading again?' On the other side write down the alternative ways of thinking that you think are helpful. Use the back of the card to summarize the work you have done, and to remind yourself of other ways of thinking, and of things that have happened that go against your old patterns of thinking. Carry the card with you at all times. Then you can use it whenever you need: when going out to do something difficult; as you arrive somewhere and before you go in to do whatever you have come to do; after you leave and before the undermining post mortem begins; or just to give yourself a much-needed boost if your confidence feels as if it is flagging.

KEY POINTS

- Thoughts affect how you feel, and feelings affect how you think. Changing the way you think will help you to feel better. There are many different kinds of thoughts, many of which most people never have to express in words.

- The first step is to identify the ways you think.

- Some patterns of thinking reflect biases. Biased ways of thinking are unlikely to be right. Many of us have 'favourite' biases, and if you know what they are it will be easier to work against them.

- The second step is to look for alternative ways of thinking.

- Good alternatives can usually be expressed in moderate or balanced terms.

- Doubting yourself and saying 'Yes, but . . .' makes finding alternatives difficult.

- It is easier to find alternatives if you use the kind of compassionate, understanding and encouraging approach that you would adopt if you were helping someone else.

- Completing thought records is extremely helpful. Although the exercises in this chapter can be done in your head, they will be much more effective and much more useful to you in the long run if you also practise doing them on paper.

- Copies of the three thought records used in this chapter can be found in the Appendix.

- Summarize the work you do on a flashcard, and use it as a reminder of new and more helpful ways of thinking.

8

Doing things differently

The last chapter explained how to find out more about the way you think about the situations that you find difficult, and how to go about keeping your thinking in perspective. This chapter is about finding out what happens when you do things differently. It explains how to test your thoughts out in action, and how to carry out experiments that help you to behave in the ways that you would like to be able to. Thinking about the things that you do differently, about how they go and what they mean, helps to build your social confidence and to reduce social anxiety. Thoughts, feelings and behavior are closely linked. If you *think* that you do not fit in well with the people around you, then you may *feel* dispirited, and *do* what you can to ensure that you only make relatively superficial contact with them. So it is important to *act* differently as well as to find different ways of *thinking*. The two together will help you to *feel* better.

Experimenting with new ways of doing things, such as being more outgoing, asking more questions, or making the effort to meet new people, allows you to discover whether other ways of thinking might be more realistic and more helpful. Acting in new ways provides a direct test of what you think. This is especially clear when your thoughts involve predictions about what will happen next. Thinking 'I shall feel dreadful the whole time', or 'I won't be able to get my point across. I will get muddled and confused', makes you want to protect yourself. Keeping safe, by avoiding things and in other ways, means that you never know if your predictions are right. Taking the risk of doing things differently can tell you whether the predictions you were making were right or wrong. You might have been upsetting yourself for no good reason.

This is where the second strategy comes in: *doing things differently*. Most people with social anxiety want to protect themselves from the embarrassments and humiliations that they fear. So they try to keep themselves safe from disaster, and they avoid doing the things that make them feel most at risk and their lives become restricted. Often the way they are thinking makes this seem like the only sensible option. Safety behaviors and avoidance are understandable reactions to feeling anxious, but in the long run they maintain the difficulty rather than resolve it. Dealing with thoughts is a beginning, but changing your behavior is essential if you are going to put your new ideas into effect.

What would changing your behavior mean?

In order to gain the most from this chapter it is important to recognize the ways in which being socially anxious or shy affect your behavior. Various ways of doing this are described below, but first read through the following passage, answering the questions it poses as you go.

Think of something you would like to do, but are inhibited from doing at present because of being socially anxious. Some examples may help you start thinking along the right lines: make the first move towards getting to know someone better; ask someone you do not know well to do something with you; look for a new job; disagree with someone in authority; make requests such as asking someone to help you out, or turn their music down, or give you the pay rise you deserve; invite people into your home; accept the offer of further training or a position with more responsibility or a promotion; or take advantage of an opportunity to stretch yourself and acquire a new skill. Use these questions as prompts to clarify where your potential lies.

1 What exactly would you be able to do if you felt less anxious?

Then ask yourself what gets in the way of doing things that you would like to do, and prevents you realizing this potential. At one level the answer is probably 'my social anxiety'. But at another level it is also because of what these situations mean to you. This is what keeps you thinking about them as sources of potential embarrassment and humiliation, and makes them seem too risky to attempt. It is as if trying to do them would put too much at stake. Something might go wrong. The dangers and threats are inhibiting and hold you back. The meaning that they have for you interferes with the way you would otherwise behave.

2 If you did try them, what do you predict would go wrong?

The inhibition that prevents you realizing your potential reflects the way you think and has a powerful effect on what you do. When something seems threatening then you think about how to protect yourself, and the two main ways of doing this are by keeping yourself safe and by avoiding things. Giving up safety behaviors and avoidance, when done in the ways described below, helps you to find out whether the threats were sufficiently serious to warrant this degree of protection. It has the potential to change their meaning for you, and in this way continues the process of change that was begun by working on your thoughts.

3 If your prediction was wrong, and things consistently turned out better than you feared they might, what would it mean to you? What would it mean about you?

Answering these three questions is intended to make you think about what you would be able to do if you were not so anxious or shy, and about what it would mean if you could, so that when you follow through the ideas below and start to change what you do, you also follow through these changes by thinking about their implications. Changing your behavior and doing things that you find difficult is important, but it is most effective if you stop and think about what you have done afterwards. Your courage in doing something that you thought would be difficult will be best rewarded, and most likely to release you from inhibition, if you follow the steps for changing your behavior that are set out below, and think about your answers to these three questions again from time to time.

The reason why this is necessary is that many people who are socially anxious go on doing things that they fear even when they feel terrible, like going to places where they will meet new people, or eating in other people's houses, but find that doing so has no lasting effect. They want to realize their potential and to be themselves, and they hope, correctly, that not doing these things is likely to make them worse. But often such courage is not rewarded, as the problem persists despite it. One reason for this is that the courageous action, or change in behavior on its own, has no profound implications for you. It does not change your expectations and predictions about what might happen next time unless you work on these too. You can always dismiss the occasional success as a lucky break, or assume that other people rather than you were responsible for its successful aspects. Courage can be turned to more profitable use if you go through all four of the steps described below when changing your behavior, so that you can test out your predictions as you go, and make your changes maximally informative. Eventually this will give new meaning to your interactions with other people – and indeed to the times when these interactions do not go according to plan.

Ways of doing things differently: mini-experiments

No special skills are needed to change your behavior. It is not as if you have to learn a whole new language, but more like finding a way of releasing you from inhibition, so that you can be yourself and feel more comfortable with that. The two main ways of behaving differently are giving up safety behaviors, and facing things rather than avoiding them; and the main method that helps you decide how to do things differently is to carry out *mini-experiments*. To do this all you need to be able to do is to be curious about what happens when you do things differently. In the rest of this chapter you will find a detailed description of exactly what to do, but first it may be useful to have an outline of the main experimental method of changing your behavior.

Adopting an experimental approach to what you do involves trying things out in different ways in order to find out what happens when you do things differently – how other people react, how you feel, and so on. The four main steps are shown in Box 8.1 below, and the next sections of this chapter will show how they can be used in practice to change safety behaviors and avoidance.

BOX 8.1: STEPS IN A MINI-EXPERIMENT FOR DOING THINGS DIFFERENTLY

With a particular situation in mind:

1 Identify exactly what you do now (your safety behaviors, what you avoid etc.).
2 Identify the connection between what you do and what you think: for example, identify your predictions, expectations, thoughts, attitudes, beliefs, assumptions, memories . . . etc.
3 Do something differently, in order to find out what happens when you do. The aim is to use your curiosity, as well as your courage.
4 Evaluate what happens. Think about it afterwards, with an open mind, and work out whether your thoughts were right.

How to do this in practice is described below.

Changing safety behaviors

As was discussed earlier, one of the difficulties about social situations is that you cannot control other people. At any moment they may do something that you find threatening, like ask your opinion, or introduce you to the person you feel least able to talk to, or move away while you are talking to them. Safety behaviors are things that you do to protect yourself from such threats. They decrease confidence in the long run because they leave you with the message that you *need* protection: that you would be unsafe without it. For example, if you had not looked away you might have given the impression that you had something to say when all you could think about was the complete blank inside.

Using safety behaviors also has the effect of suggesting that they worked: that they succeeded in preventing the threat being realized, or the disaster happening. So when you looked away you effectively moved out of the conversation, leaving other people to take it up. No one seemed to realize how blank you felt as the conversation went on – leaving you behind perhaps, but without making you the focus of a social awkwardness, an embarrassing silence.

Safety behaviors, like letting your hair fall in front of your face, or smoking so as to have something to do with your hands, keep the problem going as they prevent you learning that the disasters you fear are more imagined than real. They can also make the situation worse, especially when they become noticeable, or if they provoke a reaction from others. For example, trying not to draw attention to yourself by speaking quietly may mean that someone asks you to repeat what you have just said, so you have to say it again more loudly, with everyone listening. In the same way, saying nothing personal about yourself, so that you keep the 'real you' hidden, can make people curious about you – especially if they want to be friendly – so they start asking probing questions.

Everyone invents their own safety behaviors, so only you know exactly what you do. Some common examples include looking down so no one can catch your eye, wearing light clothing in case you get hot and sweaty, leaving the room immediately the meeting is over so that you do not have to get involved in 'small talk', and trying to be especially careful about what you say, or to make sure that it makes sense. Many socially anxious people keep an eye on the escape route when they feel uncomfortable, and arm themselves ahead of time with excuses for getting away. Most of them also try not to attract unwanted attention. You will find more examples in Chapter 1, on page 12.

Steps towards giving up safety behaviors

There are four steps to go through, and all four together make up a mini-experiment. The first is becoming aware of what you do to protect yourself. The second is thinking about exactly what could go wrong. It specifies the danger from which the safety behavior would protect you, and involves identifying what you predict would happen if you did not do it. The third step is to find out what happens if you do things differently. The last step is drawing conclusions from what you have done. These steps are described in more detail below.

STEP 1: IDENTIFYING WHAT YOU DO

In order to solve the problem of safety behaviors you need first to become aware of them. This is not so easy as it might seem, as some of them may be so habitual that you no longer notice them. There may be things that only you know you are doing, like rehearsing in advance what you want to say, or ones that others can see, like wearing the 'right' sorts of clothes. There are likely to be things that you do not do as well as things that you do: for example, talking about yourself and your feelings, or telling a story or a joke. It is particularly helpful to give yourself prompts when identifying your safety behaviors.

So think about a recent situation that you found difficult, and ask yourself what you did to ensure that you did not feel too vulnerable or exposed. You might also find it useful to think about what would have made the situation worse for you, like having to talk without notes, or not being able to have a drink before you went out. Using 'props' is a common way of keeping safe.

Write down all the safety behaviors you can think of, and keep adding to the list as you become more aware of what you do. Do some people provide a 'reassuring presence' for you, so that just having them in the vicinity makes you feel better? Do you use them as part of your safety system?

Key questions for identifying safety behaviors

- What do you do to prevent bad things happening?
- How do you protect yourself from the social embarrassments that you fear?
- If you feel suddenly at risk, what is the first thing you do?
- What do you do to prevent other people noticing your symptoms?
- What do you do to ensure that you do not do anything wrong?
- What do you do to hide your problem or to stop it showing?

STEP 2: MAKING A PREDICTION

Step 2 involves thinking about what would happen if you gave up your safety behaviors, and stopped trying to protect yourself. You can identify your predictions best by thinking about specific times and events when you have felt bad. Pick a particular one that you can remember clearly. Or start by thinking about something that might happen quite soon, and ask yourself what you fear might happen to you. There are many questions you could ask yourself at this stage: for example, *What are you predicting will happen? What is it that you fear will go wrong for you? What would happen if you did not protect yourself?* But the most important *key question* to answer is this one:

What is the worst thing that could happen to you?

Make sure that you let yourself 'look into the abyss' and try to put into words the catastrophe that you predict will happen. Write it down, to make sure that you know exactly what it is. Sometimes your worst fear, on inspection, sounds not too bad when brought out into the open, and sometimes it sounds so extreme that you can immediately see that is it not likely to be correct – like thinking that everyone will openly point at you, or laugh at you. Other predictions have more reality behind them. Someone who let her hair fall in front of her face to hide her blushes feared that people would ridicule her – as indeed her school friends once had – if they saw her hot, red face glowing like a beacon when someone spoke to her. Someone else who kept trying to tell jokes at work feared that he would be rejected and become totally isolated if he did not join in the general banter.

Think about how to word your predictions so that they are testable. Predictions about yourself are perhaps the easiest to test: 'I shall shake, and spill my drink', 'My anxiety will get out of control'. Predictions about other people need to be specific if they are going to be testable. You might predict that other people will stare at you, or that they will ignore you. These predictions can be tested, but no experiments are likely to reveal exactly what other people think of you. Predictions about other people's thoughts and attitudes are hardest to tackle. Predictions about their behavior are much easier. In order to test a prediction about being rejected and becoming totally isolated, for example, you would first have to work out how you would know if this was happening. You would have to define the *objective* signs of being rejected, and be sure that you were not using signs, like someone turning away from you, or yawning, as signs of rejection. These things could happen for so many other reasons that the signs are not objectively clear, and leave too much room for you to give your own personal and anxiety-driven meaning to them, about being rejected or becoming totally isolated. So in this case it would be better to test the specific prediction that you will feel rejected, or that other people will not start conversations with you, or that they will not respond to your comments, look you in the eye, or ask you to join them and so on.

When people predict other people's reactions to them, for example predicting that they will not take them seriously, it is especially difficult to make the prediction testable.

How would you know whether people took you seriously? How would anyone know? You could decide what would count as *not* being taken seriously, and define specific criteria for that, like never listening to what you say, or always ignoring your opinion. But definitions that use 'extremist' words, like 'never' and 'always' are only rarely likely to be true (see page 149). The point here is that sometimes the attempt to look for specific predictions itself reveals that the prediction is so general – or so *over-general* – that it is most unlikely to be correct. It will be most helpful if you make specific predictions that seem realistic to you. Then testing them out will tell you something you did not already know.

STEP 3: FIND OUT WHAT HAPPENS IF YOU GIVE UP USING YOUR SAFETY BEHAVIORS

This is the point at which you have to think about how to change your behavior: about the kind of mini-experiment you will carry out. Think first of a situation in which you would like things to be different, such as using the telephone when other people are listening, or starting a conversation with someone. What will you do differently? Be quite specific about it. You should choose one of the safety behaviors on your list and create an experiment for yourself, to test out what happens if you go into this situation 'unprotected': for example, if you look people in the eye when you talk to them instead of avoiding eye contact, or say what you think instead of just agreeing with them; if you relax your grip on the telephone or the pencil or the coffee mug instead of tensing yourself up in an effort to control the shaking. The aim is to find out if the danger you fear is real, and in order to do this you need to drop your armour and see if the disaster you fear comes to pass.

This is the hardest step, and the one that feels most risky at first. It is worth doing because it starts the process of building up confidence in your ability to adapt to the situations that arise and to respond to them in the way that feels right for you. If you feel anxious the first time you do it, try again and see if by degrees your anxiety starts to die down.

A reminder: there is no fixed, rigid and right way of doing things socially, but there are many ways. Your way, once you have learned to relax and to be yourself, will be just as good as the next person's. Trying to keep yourself safe tends to make you more tense and inflexible than you otherwise would be. Giving up your safety behaviors, once you have got used to doing without them, allows you to adapt as the situation unfolds, and frees you up to interact in new and more natural ways, even though it feels alarming at first. The person who tried to hide her blushes carried out the experiment of tying back her hair and holding her head up straight, in full view of everyone around her. The person who kept trying to tell jokes tried keeping quiet until he had something to say instead.

STEP 4: EVALUATE WHAT HAPPENS

Think about what actually happened when you behaved differently. Make sure that you are sticking with the facts and not jumping to conclusions about what other people thought, or assuming that because you felt anxious you did something stupid or revealed your basic weaknesses. Ask yourself: Did the prediction come true? Were you right? Or were you misled by your anxiety? Seeing things in an alarming light whose shade was determined by your fear rather than the facts? In the Appendix you will find a 'Thought record for changing behaviors'. Fill in one of these, using the example shown in Table 8.2 to guide you, in order to bring your experiment to a useful conclusion. Although you may be able to do this in your head, it takes a surprising amount of practice to do it accurately and well, and the worksheet will help you to make the most of the experiments that you do.

What if the worst thing happens?

Dropping safety behaviors will feel risky. It will take courage, because it always seems possible that the thing you fear most will really happen. There are two answers to this problem. First, the thing that you fear very rarely does happen. Indeed, it is more likely to happen if you keep using the safety behavior than if you give it up. For example, the person who kept trying to hide her blushes was inadvertently drawing attention to herself when she tried to hide. She attracted the attention she was trying to evade, and this made her more likely to blush. When she stopped trying to hide, and let the blushes come and go as they pleased, she realized that other people took their cue from her. They too paid little attention to the blushes, and continued to interact with her in a perfectly normal way. And the person who stopped trying to tell jokes and keep up the banter with his colleagues at work quickly realized that the tense and nervous jokes he usually contributed had mostly fallen flat. They were more likely to invite the ridicule that he feared than allowing himself to be the quiet person that he really was.

TABLE 8.2: THOUGHT RECORD FOR CHANGING BEHAVIORS

Specific situation (Think of a situation in which you use a safety behavior)	Prediction (What will happen if you do not keep yourself safe? How will you know if it happens?)	Experiment (How will you find out? What will you do differently?)	What actually happened? (What did you observe? Stick to the facts.)	Conclusions (What does this mean?)
Hiding my face when someone in the office asks me a question	I will blush and go bright red. They will look away, and stop talking to me.	I will stop hiding myself, stay in full view, and let them see what happens.	I did go red. But I did not hide, and the conversation just went on.	That going red is not as disastrous as I feared. That I don't need to hide.
A pause in the conversation when I start talking nonsense just to fill in the gap	The silence will go on, and no one will speak. My anxiety will get out of control, and become visible to everyone.	I will try saying nothing, and waiting for someone else to break the silence.	I did feel highly anxious, but everyone else just went on talking when they were ready.	I'm not the only one responsible for keeping things going.
Going out at a time when I am unlikely to meet, or have to talk to, people I know	People will approach me, and say something that I should answer. I will feel nervous, and say something stupid.	I will go out at busier times, answer if someone speaks to me, and not cross the street to avoid anyone.	I felt very nervous, but I answered someone who said 'Good morning'. OK. I passed someone I knew, but they said nothing.	I suppose I could get used to it. People don't seem to be that interested in talking anyway, in those circumstances.

Secondly, if the thing that you fear most does happen, then it may not have the catastrophic implications that you assume it does. Imagine you have kept yourself safe by never letting anyone know what you feel, and by not saying what you really think. Then you decide to take your courage in both hands, and to disclose something important about yourself to someone you respect, and they seem to dismiss you and your feelings, or they seem bored and uninterested. Ask yourself: How would you know what they thought? And what they felt? Or what their reactions meant? Could they have misunderstood what you said? Or were they being insensitive because they did not realize how important it was for you? The fact is that often other people do not respond in the ways that one hopes that they will, but there are many reasons for this. Socially anxious people tend to take such happenings personally, and to mind read, but other people's unhelpful or insensitive reactions do not make you less acceptable as a person, or make your feelings less important and meaningful.

Facing the fears by stopping avoiding things

Avoidance is not doing something because it makes you fearful or anxious. It is one of the more extreme versions of keeping safe. There are many kinds of avoidance, and some of them are easier to recognize than others. Examples of obvious types of avoidance include not going to places where you know you will meet people, not using the telephone, not eating in public or asking questions, not speaking to strangers, not asking someone out for a date, refusing invitations and so on.

More subtle types of avoidance are so familiar, and so

much part and parcel of the way people behave when they are socially anxious, that they are not even aware of doing them. They include not starting conversations or not initiating contact with people; not accepting a challenge; or never doing things on your own. Some people become very good at skimming the surface of social situations, and might make a habit of arriving at them late and leaving early. At a party you could still avoid talking to people by helping with the food and drink, or with the clearing up, and find a way of only half paying attention to other people. One person with severe social phobia described this as being 'both there and not there', and for him it happened whenever he was with a group of people who were talking among themselves. He wanted to be part of the conversation, and to feel that he belonged to the group and was accepted by them, but still disengaged himself, and felt detached for much of the time. Perhaps you know what he meant.

Experiments for facing things rather than avoiding them

The same four steps can be used to plan how to face rather than avoid the things that you find difficult:

1 Identify what you avoid.
2 Identify the connection between what you avoid and what you think.
3 Do something differently: in this case, face the fear rather than avoid it.
4 Evaluate what happens. Think about what happened, as objectively as you can. Then work out whether your thoughts about what might happen were right.

The first step sounds relatively easy, and often it is. However, when thinking about precisely what you avoid, remember that you are probably the only person who knows exactly what that is, and how you manage to avoid it. Try to notice when you feel like avoiding something, and when you get that sense of wanting to withdraw or hide yourself away that leads to avoidance. A good test of whether you are avoiding something or not is to ask: 'If I were confident, would I do it?'

The second step, identifying the part played in your avoidance by the way you think, means asking yourself what you predict, or expect might happen if you did it. What is your worst fear? Do you have any memories or images about similar situations that explain why they seem to you to be so alarming? The key questions for identifying thoughts may be useful here; see Chapter 7, page 134.

The third step, acting so as to face the fear rather than avoiding it, is always the hardest, and often it helps to build your confidence up by doing easier things before you move on to harder ones. So you could start by greeting people when you meet them and build up to full-length conversations. Or you could start by listening to others and watching what they do, and build up to asking someone out for a date. Or you could involve yourself in helpful activities in your local neighbourhood, or join an evening class, as a step on the way to making more personal relationships and better friendships. Your aim should be to be able to do the thing that you are avoiding.

The fourth step has two parts: observing what actually happened, and working out how this fits with what you originally thought, or what your observations mean. It is only too easy to dismiss or to discount the things that happen as a result of carrying out experiments, especially if nothing in particular goes wrong. If you managed to do something new for you, like make an appointment to get your hair cut, then it is easy to think of this as the kind of normal activity that *should* present you with no particular problems. This is why it is so important to identify your original thoughts, for example your expectations and predictions, before you go ahead and do something that you might not otherwise do. Doing it this way puts you in a position to find out whether your expectations, or predictions, are confirmed or not. For example, you might expect to feel embarrassed and humiliated by having to watch yourself in the mirror while having your hair cut, or predict that the person cutting your hair will make a personal remark about you, or ask you personal questions. If you know exactly what you expect to happen, you can find out whether your expectations are confirmed or were wrong. In this way, doing things differently can help to change the way you think as well as to change what you do. So next time your expectations and predictions, based on your new findings, should be different.

Keeping records of your experiments

Keep a written record of the risks that you take, and of what happens at the time, in your notebook. Otherwise you will not know how you are getting on. It is surprising how easy it is to forget, especially when a success for you (using the telephone when people can hear what you say) may feel like normality for someone else. A written record allows you to see clearly what you are changing, and it helps you plan what to do next.

Other kinds of experiment

Using experiments to guide you, when you decide to do something differently, is a way of making the most of everything that you do, so that the changes in how you think, feel and act fit together. When this happens your confidence will grow more quickly. For this reason it is worth being as creative and imaginative as you can when thinking up experiments to change your behavior. We have focused here on how to change safety behaviors and how to face things instead of avoiding them, but there are also other kinds of experiments you could do. For example, you could go to some places as an observer, instead of a participant, and notice what other people do, and whether any of them show signs of being anxious or shy. Or you could experiment with the way you make use of the basic elements of social interaction, such as listening to other people, looking at them, working out what they feel about what they are saying, asking questions when you want to find out about others, saying what you think, expressing your feelings and so on. These are all ways of oiling the wheels of social communication that help people to join in with others, and give them a better sense of belonging rather than feeling like an outsider. Experiment with doing them more and with doing them less than usual, to find out what effect this has.

Another experiment that is particularly informative for people who fear that their symptoms will be noticed – and think that it matters when they are – is intentionally to make the symptoms worse. So you could make yourself shake visibly, or stumble over your words when saying something, or repeat yourself on purpose, and then observe what happens. Identify your prediction first: the catastrophe that you fear. Then use your observation to find out whether your prediction was right. This is particularly hard to do for people who believe that there is a right – and therefore a wrong – way of doing things, and that their way is bound to be wrong, but for them, it is also particularly helpful.

Should you be trying to learn how to do things right?

In a way shyness and social anxiety are all about what you do: about what you fear you might do, or might not do. The fear is that you will *act* in a way that will be humiliating or embarrassing, or *do something* that reveals your symptoms of anxiety; that you will *behave* in a way that is unacceptable, or *do* something wrong – knock something over, or blurt out something personal at an inappropriate moment. The fear of showing yourself up by the way you act is inhibiting, and prevents you behaving as you otherwise would. But focusing on changing behaviors is not about learning how to 'do things right'. Nor is it about learning how to behave so that 'bad' things do not happen to you. Nothing you can do will guarantee protection from the occasional rejection, or moment when you feel embarrassed and painfully conspicuous. Everyone has times when they cannot think of anything of any interest to say to anyone; when they are undeniably boring. Social awkwardnesses will continue to plague us all, but the *meaning* of them can change. They can come to feel less dangerous and threatening. They can be less inhibiting, and have less devastating implications for one's personal sense of adequacy or acceptability – becoming more like making a trivial mistake such as leaving your umbrella behind or running out of toothpaste.

Changing behaviors has a powerful effect partly because it allows you to do the things that you want to do, and also because it can help to change meanings. Carrying out behavioral experiments such as the ones described in this chapter allows you to re-evaluate social threats and dangers so that they come to have a different meaning for you. They make it possible to find out whether your more anxious predictions and expectations, for example about how you might embarrass or humiliate yourself, are correct. Changing what you do is another way of finding out whether taking another viewpoint, or adopting another standpoint, helps you to feel more confident in the ways that you interact with others. So changing your behavior also helps you to realize your potential and to be yourself in a less inhibited way.

A digression about conventions

Some people think that in order to get better they should learn how to behave correctly, as if there were a right way of doing things. Indeed, there are some situations in which the conventional ways of doing things are rather like rules, and then it can certainly feel more comfortable to know what the rules are: for example, how to order a meal, make an appointment to see the doctor, or do what is expected of you as a member of a sports club or church or evening class or committee. Learning the rules in such situations has been described as being like learning a 'script'. The script is useful because it tells you how to behave, but rule books are not written with flexibility in mind. Sometimes it is not possible to use the usual script even though you would like to, for example when someone starts a personal conversation with you at work, or if you meet your doctor in the supermarket.

Rules and scripts are helpful, but they can also be limiting. An efficient and busy hotel receptionist who suffered from social anxiety had remarkably little difficulty carrying out her job. She had been well trained, and had been told exactly how to handle the various types of problems that arose in her work, including dealing with complaints and untoward rudeness. She had been able to rehearse and practise all the skills that she needed on the job, and applying these skills was merely a matter of following the rules. There was nothing personal about it. Indeed, she could do the job regardless of how she was feeling at the time, as it had become rather like switching into automatic, and putting on her professional mask.

But although she knew her 'script' well, without it she felt, literally, 'unmasked'. In more personal situations, when there were no rules to guide her, she felt at sea and at risk. She was deeply embarrassed by not being able to think what to say to a colleague whom she met when out for a walk at the weekend. Her first attempts to overcome the problem involved looking for the rules of the game: hunting for a 'script' that would help her out. But more personal, and especially more intimate, relationships develop their own conventions, so to speak, which means that you may not always know exactly what to do ahead of time. It is rather that one has to learn to do what feels right, and to respond flexibly to the demands of the situation as it develops. So this chapter is intended to help you to develop the confidence to adapt the way you behave to the situation that you find yourself in. The emphasis is therefore on thinking about how to realize your potential rather than look for rules or conventions, which in their own way can inhibit your ability to express yourself in the way that feels right to you.

No special skills are needed to be able to do this. It comes without teaching, and is more a matter of feeling able to be yourself, and finding the ways of doing so that work for you rather than against you. There are some special skills – 'advanced skills', so to speak – that it can be helpful to learn, and these are often described in books to help people progress further in their business or management careers. Some of these are explained in Part Three. You already have all the skills that you need for using the ideas in this chapter, although it is certainly possible that when you are feeling anxious it is hard to use them in the ways that you otherwise would.

Taking risks and making mistakes

Changing behaviors involves taking risks, and one of the things that holds people back is the fear of making mistakes. This will seem more risky if you think that mistakes matter: if you think that the mistakes you make will make others think badly of you, or make you conspicuous (however temporarily). But everyone makes mistakes, most of which are invisible to anyone but themselves, and most mistakes have no more significance than tripping over a kerbstone. Most of them turn out to be useful, too, as you can learn something from them, like to look where you are going more carefully. So experiments done in the ways described here help you to break the vicious cycles that otherwise keep the problem going, help you to do more of the things that you would like to do, and help you to feel more comfortable about doing them. They work by providing a new source of information, which helps you to think again about these mistakes, or ways in which you suppose that your behavior might have been wrong.

Some general points about doing things differently

Keep going

When it comes to changing their behavior, some people give up because they do not consider that they have made any progress. This can happen even though other people see a change. Take care not to underrate your achievements. Watch out for upsetting thoughts about your progress. Progress may seem slow at first but it will gradually become more substantial and more noticeable to you. If it was easy, you would have done it before. You might also find it much easier to remember the things that went badly than those that went well, or those that just felt normal. Perhaps the difficult times seem more important, as well as more distressing, than the easy ones, which then get forgotten.

Acknowledge your achievements

If you learn how to praise yourself for your successes, your confidence will grow faster. Each time you achieve something it is a success. Small successes turn into larger successes. Give yourself credit for all of them. Make a habit of giving yourself a mental pat on the back, and see if you can get someone else to notice your achievements. If you have a colleague, friend or relative who knows about your difficulties, maybe you could tell them, as well as writing it all down in your notebook. Most people underrate their achievements to start with. This is particularly likely to happen if the risks you decide to take involve doing things that most people seem to find easy, like ordering a meal, or saying no when someone asks you to do something.

Here are some examples of how people downgrade their successes. Below each of these upsetting thoughts you will find an example of the sort of answer that might be more helpful.

Thought: 'Yes, but anyone could do that.'
Answer: 'Not if they felt as anxious as you.'
Thought: 'I should have done it better.'
Answer: 'I will, in time. Now I will do what I can. No one could do more than that.'
Thought: 'No one else would think that was important.'
Answer: 'Maybe not. But I know how important it is to me.'

Downgrading your success makes you feel bad, and it makes it hard to keep trying.

Upsetting thoughts, as already mentioned, affect both your feelings and your behavior. Make sure you know how to deal with them. Encouragement works far better than criticism because it makes you feel better and helps you to keep trying. So encourage yourself as you would encourage anyone who was learning how to do something new. Try not to criticize or undermine yourself. If doing new things makes you more anxious, then remember that this kind of anxiety is highly likely to be temporary, and the gains you make will last if you keep on doing them.

Dealing with setbacks

Everyone has 'ups and downs', and what you did success-fully yesterday may seem impossible today. It is important to realize that setbacks are a normal part of progress and that you need not be discouraged by them.

If at any stage you seem to be stuck, or even to have slid backwards, it could be because you are trying to run before you can walk. Recognize that you may have to take things slowly, and that breaking old patterns of thinking and of behaving takes time. Sometimes you will find the old ways of keeping yourself safe re-emerge, but what can change once can do so again. Even a small change means that you are not stuck with the problem, but need to keep working on it. Watch out for feeling discouraged, and use your new thinking skills to keep the setback in perspective. Everyone should expect a few setbacks, so when they happen to you try to take them in your stride, and do not let them inter-fere with your plans. If you do not give up you will over-come the problem in the end.

Setbacks are often more apparent than real. You may have a bad day because you were tired or not very well. It is not that you have got worse, but rather that being tired or unwell makes everything you do a bit harder. Or other people may unexpectedly plunge you into a situation that you were not yet ready for. For instance they might suggest that you come with them to a disco, or ask you to explain why you disagreed with a decision made at work. Remember that other people are far less aware of your anxiety than you are. They may not even notice it at all. So try not to let a bad patch spread. If you need time to take stock, to muster your strength and your energy, then take that time before you continue making the changes that you find most difficult.

Adopting an 'ever ready' attitude

If keeping yourself safe keeps the problem going, then taking risks helps to overcome it. So take every opportunity that arises and, for instance, go to the pub or talk to someone in a bus queue if you have an unexpected chance to do so. You will find, if you can do this, both that you will improve faster and that ordinary everyday activities become less of a strain. You will no longer react to them as if they were really dangerous or frightening.

Try to stop keeping yourself safe even when doing everyday tasks, and instead of buying what you want without a word, deliberately talking to shop assistants or cashiers instead. Look at ordinary activities to see if you can find a way of turning them into useful ways of making progress.

What if taking risks, and doing things differently, makes me very anxious?

You will not be able to overcome the problem without experiencing some degree of anxiety, but the more confident you become the more quickly this will diminish. Think of handling your anxiety differently at different times: before, during or after taking the risk of doing something differently.

Beforehand

Once you have decided to go ahead and do something difficult it is sensible not to keep dwelling on it. It is not wise to give free rein to your imagination when thoughts or images of potential disasters come to mind. These will only make you feel worse, and it is more helpful to stick with your decision to act, and then to distract yourself in any way you can to stop yourself worrying about it. Keep yourself as busy and occupied as possible. You will find more ideas about how to do this in Chapter 9.

After the event

Try to stop yourself going in for a 'post mortem'. Looking back at what happened from the point of view of someone with social phobia, it is only too easy to interpret everything that happened in terms of your own sense of failure, inadequacy or distress. Post mortems of this kind are as unlikely to be accurate as exaggerated 'fishy' stories about the size of the one that got away.

At the time

The key to coping with your feelings at the time is to pay less attention to them. The aim is to focus more on what is happening around you and less on your internal thoughts, feelings and self appraisals. The third strategy for overcoming social phobia, reducing self-consciousness, explains how to do this, and this is the subject of the next chapter.

KEY POINTS

- Doing things differently is one of the most productive ways to build your confidence.
- The way to do this is to think of yourself as carrying out small experiments, to find out what happens when you change your behavior.
- Experiments can help you give up using safety behaviors which otherwise keep the problems going.
- Facing things instead of avoiding them also breaks one of the cycles of maintenance, and experimenting with doing this makes it easier to do.
- There are many ways in which experiments can help you to change your behavior, and you might be able to think of more ways for yourself.
- It is less important to worry about whether you will do things wrong, or break a social convention, than to start doing things in the way that you really would like to.
- When thinking back on the things that you have done differently it is important not to dismiss or discount your successes. Doing new things may make you more anxious at first, but it will also help to build your confidence in the long run.

9

Reducing self-consciousness

Self-consciousness comes from focusing your attention inwards, on to yourself, so that you become painfully aware of what is happening to you. At its worst, self-consciousness dominates your attention and makes it difficult to think of anything else but your inner experience – and this can become totally paralyzing. A bout of self-consciousness can afflict you in any social situation, regardless of how well you know the people you are with. Entering a room full of people, or saying goodbye when you leave, appear to be situations which are especially likely to provoke it, possibly because at those times it is more difficult to do what is expected of you socially without drawing attention to yourself.

Self-consciousness goes with feeling conspicuous and, for socially anxious people, that goes with feeling vulnerable. It can be provoked, or made worse, by becoming aware of any of the symptoms of social anxiety. For example, not being able to concentrate or think straight, feeling nervous, noticing how hot you are, hearing the sound of your own voice, having the impression that you are being scrutinized, doing something clumsy, catching a glimpse of your hand movements, worrying about some aspect of your appearance or your performance could all make you feel self-conscious.

The less self-conscious you are, the easier it is to be yourself, and to join in spontaneously with what is going on around you. The most helpful strategy to learn in order to become less self-conscious is how to direct your attention on to other things, so that you break the pattern of inward focusing which makes you so self-aware. The idea is that if you can 'lose yourself' or 'forget yourself', you will be better able to 'find yourself' – to be your 'real self' and feel comfortable being that way. The assumption behind using these familiar phrases here is that there is nothing new or special that you have to learn in order to be able to interact more naturally with other people, because things will work out fine if only you can manage to become less self-conscious about it. When watching a gripping film, or when studying a timetable in order to decide which train to catch, concentrating on what you are doing means that you notice little else. The cinema may be draughty and the rail station crowded and noisy, but these things are irrelevant to what you are doing, and can go completely unnoticed until you disengage yourself, and give them some of your attention. If you gave other people, and things outside yourself, a similar degree of attention there would be less space left for noticing the discomfort and tumult inside.

The effects of self-consciousness

Feeling self-conscious makes all kinds of symptoms worse: the sensations themselves, the need for self-protection and to resort to using safety behaviors, the inability to act naturally and numerous kinds of socially anxious thinking. At the same time it serves as a *reminder* of how unpleasant the symptoms are and increases the fear that others will notice them. It *focuses attention* on what others might think and on the fear of how they might react, and it makes you feel *uncertain and unconfident*. All of these reactions make it difficult to become fully involved in particular situations or social interactions. As the mind is occupied with internally generated information, the capacity left over for picking up other kinds of information is limited, and what does get through tends to be hazy, insufficient or inaccurate. This is one reason why being self-conscious interferes with the ability to carry out ordinary activities in a natural and smooth way, so that your elbow knocks the flowers from the table, or your tie lands in the soup, or you hesitate when greeting someone between the handshake and the kiss, and suddenly feel that you do not know what you are expected to say or do, or where to put yourself.

We know this is happening from research as well as from what people say about their anxiety. Researchers have found that socially anxious people remember fewer details of the situations they have been in compared with other people, and also that they rate other people's facial expressions more negatively than others do. It is as if they know a great deal about themselves, but rather less about things outside themselves, and use their socially anxious imagination when they fill in the gaps. Socially anxious people tend to measure the degree of risk involved in a particular situation not in terms of social factors such as what might happen, or who might be there, but in terms of how they might feel. Also, the worse they feel the more dangerous the situation seems to be. Internal information becomes the measure of the amount of risk involved.

In terms of the model described in Chapter 5, and shown on page 84, self-consciousness is at the centre of all the main vicious cycles that keep social anxiety going, and some complex, real-life examples of these cycles are provided next. These have been chosen to illustrate how, much of the time, the effects of self-consciousness do not come separately, but are mixed up together. When you read through the examples, try to notice the many different ways in which feeling self-conscious works to keep the problem going.

James and his girlfriend were going to have a meal with her parents. He did not know them well yet, and as soon as they walked in at the door he thought to himself that they were sizing him up. Suddenly he became aware of every movement he made, and everything he thought of saying seemed to present itself for inspection before he said it – only to be censored at once. His mouth felt too dry to talk, and he felt too awkward to ask for a drink. All he could think about was his inner foolishness, and the need for the situation to come to end. 'How long is this going to last?' was the question in his mind. Then suddenly everyone was laughing, and he had clearly missed the joke. He

had the terrible thought that he must have done something odd, or said something stupid, and that they were
laughing at him. Later his girlfriend told him that no
one had noticed anything at all. Although he had been
rather quiet at first, to her this had seemed understandable – and only natural.

As Sandra came into the office the head of her department stopped as he rushed by and asked if she would
make a couple of announcements for him at their group's
early morning meeting. He had unexpectedly been called
out, and as he hurried away, he thrust a piece of paper
into her hand with something scribbled on it. Sandra
was extremely nervous about having to do this and she
knew that the longer she had to worry the worse she
would feel. So she decided to do it immediately, and
walked straight into the meeting room without even
taking her coat off. The meeting was just starting, so
she went to the front of the room, explained why she
was there and read out the first part of the message.
But the second part had been scribbled so hurriedly
that it was almost impossible to read. She hesitated,
and suddenly she heard her voice dying away. As the
silence went on she was convinced that all eyes were
upon her, standing there awkwardly, still in her over-
coat. In her mind's eye she had a vision of how she
must look. She described herself later as childish looking;
tall, shapeless like a lanky adolescent, with the bit of
paper fluttering in her trembling hands, peering at it
short-sightedly for a clue as to what it might mean. It

seemed like an eternity before she thought of explaining that she could not read his writing and passed the note to someone else. When they could do no better than she had done, her confusion died away, but only partly. The image of seeing herself as others saw her haunted her for the rest of the day. Each time it came back she was covered with confusion again, feeling hot and foolish, as if stripped of all protective armour.

Andrew was talking on the telephone when three people he knew walked into the room, talking loudly to each other. As he became aware that they could hear everything he was saying, he lowered his voice. One of them noticed this and told the others to be quieter, and in the hush that followed his voice appeared to Andrew to echo round the room. He could no longer concentrate on what he was saying, or understand properly what was being said to him. He spoke even more quietly, until he was almost whispering, and the silence around him appeared to grow. Frantically he wondered how to end the conversation, and so he made some excuse (that later he could not remember), and hung up. He was astonished when he looked up that the others were no longer there. They must have walked through the room and out the other side. It was the thought that they might have been listening and judging him that had made him so self-conscious, and had dominated his thoughts to the extent that he was unaware of anything else.

BOX 9.1: SUMMARY OF THE EFFECTS OF SELF-CONSCIOUSNESS

1 It focuses attention on to yourself so you notice:
- sensations like feeling hot;
- behaviors, like fiddling with your hands;
- emotions (or feelings), like feeling embarrassed;
- thoughts, like 'They think I'm peculiar'.

2 You tend to see yourself as you suppose others see you.

3 It makes you want to protect yourself: by keeping yourself safe or escaping from the situation.

4 It is difficult to notice other things accurately at the same time, although you may also notice some things of particular significance to you, like a fleeting expression on someone's face, without noticing much else.

5 You feel increasingly at risk, and all these effects get more pronounced, and make the problem worse, the longer they go on.

An exercise

As a way of understanding better what happens to you, and its various effects, think about some specific instances from your own experience. Try to think through one or two of them in enough detail to identify how self-consciousness makes you feel more vulnerable. It is often difficult to work out how it deprives you of accurate information about what is going on, as of course you will have no memory for the information that you never picked up in the first place, and you may have filled the gaps using your own imagination. But you may remember how, when your attention is turned inwards, it becomes difficult to follow what people are saying, to notice what they are doing, and to judge how they are *really* reacting. It is easy to suppose that they can see all the signs of anxiety and inadequacy that you feel, and to suppose that when they see them they are judging you – negatively, of course – on the basis of them. Many of the conclusions that people reach when they feel self-conscious are based on their inner experience of the feelings, sensations and actions that they find so distressing: 'I said so little, and felt so embarrassed that they could see how inadequate and useless I am.' It is as if they are so aware of these things that they suppose that other people must be so too. For each specific situation you can think of, answer these two questions:

What conclusions about yourself did you come to after a time when you felt self-conscious?
What conclusions do you think other people came to about you at the same time?

Reducing self-consciousness

The key to reducing self consciousness is to learn how to focus more of your attention on what is happening outside yourself, instead of on what is happening inside; to forget yourself enough to become absorbed in your social life instead. To do this, you need consciously to concentrate on diverting your attention away from yourself and on to other things, including the other people around you – the source of the fear. The attitude that helps you to do this is one of curiosity. Your task is to watch what happens, and to think openly about it, just as a scientist might when investigating a new field. Adopting this attitude helps you to interact with others more smoothly and more naturally. *Listen to what they say, and look at what they do before coming to a judgment about how they are reacting.* Think of yourself as exploring so as to reach a considered opinion that another dispassionate observer of the same situation would also agree with. Try to make sure that you are not relying on guesswork, as this is highly likely to be influenced by your expectations and assumptions.

Of course, this is easier said than done. As you know, when you feel bad it is difficult not to think about yourself, and to turn your attention away from your distress. Painful experiences tend to dominate our attention, and not many people could obey the instructions above without more guidance as to how to set about it. So it is helpful to think of learning to divert your attention as a two-stage process:

1 Deciding not to think about the unpleasant experiences.
2 Filling your mind with something else.

Deciding not to think about the unpleasant experiences

It would be useful for unpleasant thoughts, feelings and sensations to grab your attention if the risk involved was a real one, and you really were in some danger. So first remember that the danger is more imagined than real. If you doubt this, go back to Chapter 7, and see if you can use the thinking skills described there to help you find a new perspective: one that helps you to keep thoughts about social danger and catastrophe in perspective. Secondly, ask yourself whether there is anything to be gained by dwelling on the unpleasantness that you experience. Does it have any benefits? Does it give you any advantages? For example, do you think that it might help to prepare you for the worst? Or allow you to make your escape before the thing that you fear most actually happens? Thoughts such as these are common, but in practice focusing your attention on yourself, or self-consciousness, has far more disadvantages than advantages.

See if you can write down the advantages for you of *not* thinking about these unpleasant experiences, and make the decision to turn your attention away from them when they intrude – which undoubtedly they will, at least at first. When your heart is thumping and you cannot find the words with which to express yourself, the *disadvantage* of paying attention to your feelings is that it makes you worse: increasingly self-aware and self-conscious. Before long you just wish that the ground would open and swallow you (mercifully) up. One *advantage* of forcing yourself to focus on people and things around you is that it gives you some recovery time. Use the examples given at the start of this chapter, and the information in Box 9.1 above, to prompt you to think of more advantages for you.

Focusing on what is happening around you

The aim of this strategy is to enable you to rely less on guesswork. You should try to give more attention to the person or people with whom you are interacting, so that you can listen better to what is being said, look at the other people involved, and notice their reactions as well as your own. The aim is not to focus 100 per cent of your attention on them and to forget yourself entirely, but to be able to achieve a balance between internal and external focusing. You would not, for example, keep your eyes fixed (unnaturally) on someone else, but rather allow yourself to make eye contact and to look away just as you might if you did not feel anxious at all.

If this seems too difficult at first, then one way to make it easier might be to give yourself something to do at the same time, like the task of finding out something about the other person or people involved. Ask yourself what you think of the way they dress, or how you can tell what they are feeling, or what their occupations are. Find something about them that interests you. Imagine that you were going to describe them to someone else, and notice some of their characteristics.

When your mind wanders

When deciding not to think about unpleasant experiences, and turning your attention to something else, you may find that your attention wanders off, or appears to be grabbed once again by your internal sensations and feelings. This is entirely normal, as attention is not a static, unchanging system, but an active, dynamic one. Unless we are especially relaxed and sleepy, our attention constantly shifts, as if we were always scanning and inter-rogating our surroundings. So, even when you have made the 'right' decision, and have succeeded in making your-self focus on something outside yourself, you may find that you quickly lose the new focus. When this happens, just repeat your original plan. Turn your attention outwards again; and it may help to *think* about something external (and unthreatening), and to *do something* to help engage your attention as well. Then the two strategies described so far, changing patterns of thinking and doing things differently, can fit together with the ones introduced here for reducing self-consciousness.

The two-way experiment

The two-way experiment can help you to learn how to control what you pay attention to. It involves trying things out in two completely different, contrasting ways, and comparing what you notice and what you feel on the two occasions. It means adopting the attitude of curiosity and finding out what happens if you pay attention exclu-sively to yourself, even exaggerating what happens when you feel self-conscious, and then doing the opposite. That would mean forcing yourself to pay attention exclusively to someone else or to something outside of yourself. It takes some courage to carry out this experiment, and you need to think carefully about it before you start. Where and when could you do it? How will you explore the difference between the two occasions? An example follows.

One relatively easy way of carrying out such an experiment might be to choose a setting when you are not much involved, or even not involved at all, with the people around you, such as when standing in the supermarket queue, or sitting on a bus or train with other people nearby. First, focus on yourself. Notice all the physical sensations that you can feel. Are you hot or cold? Hungry? Tired? Can you feel your clothes? Is anything too tight or too loose? What are your feelings and emotions? Is anything particular running through your mind? Any images? Or impressions? Or memories? In order to keep up the internal focusing for long enough for the experiment to be useful you should probably continue doing this for three to five minutes. If your mind wanders, then bring it back to yourself. It is all right to let your mind wander on to your own concerns and worries, if you like, but if it wanders away from yourself then just bring it back again and keep up the internal focus.

Then ask yourself the two assessment questions: *How did you feel?* and *What did you notice?* When answering these questions you could use your curiosity as a prompt. Were you surprised by how many things were going on inside? Did you become more aware of your inner experiences? If so, did this change them in any way? Make them more or less intense? And what did you notice? Do you know anything about what the other people around you looked like? About their expressions, appearance, conversations and actions, for example? Could you describe something about one of them? Or describe exactly what one of them was doing while you were focusing on yourself? You should make sure that your answers are clear to yourself. Make a mental note of them, or even write them down, before going on with the experiment.

The next step is to reverse the experiment. For another few minutes try to focus your attention exclusively outside yourself. Notice something about each of the people around you. Without obviously staring at them, see if you can be sensitive to something about them, such as how they might feel, how lively or energetic or lethargic they seem, how physically fit they might be – anything you can think of that might be of interest to you. If it seems natural and appropriate, then talk to them. Allow yourself to get into conversation, and allow your curiosity to lead the way. Then ask yourself the two assessment questions again: *What did you feel this time?* and *What did you notice this time?* Make sure your answers are clear again, by making either a mental or a written note.

Finally, to sum up the experiment, and think about what you have learned, compare your answers to the two sets of questions. Draw some conclusions on the basis of what happened, first about the effects of focusing your attention internally, and second about the effects of focusing your attention externally. What did you do in order to use your curiosity, and focus externally? How did you do it? Could you do it again, in more demanding situations?

BOX 9.2: SUMMARY OF THE TWO-WAY EXPERIMENT

1 The internal focus: pay full attention to yourself, e.g. for three to five minutes.

2 Answer the assessment questions:
- How did you feel?
- What did you notice?

Make your answers clear to yourself. Make a mental or written note of them.

3 The external focus: pay full attention to other people, e.g. for three to five minutes.

4 Answer the assessment questions:
- How did you feel?
- What did you notice?

Make your answers clear to yourself. Make a mental or written note of them.

5 Compare the two:
- What was different?
- What was the same?

6 Summarize your conclusions:
- Which way made you feel better?
- Which way gave you more of the information that helps you along, socially?
- Was the external focus difficult to achieve? How did you do it?
- Do you need more practice to achieve the desired effect? If so, when could you try it again?

Doing a brief two-way mini-experiment when talking to someone is particularly informative, and you may need to carry out a few two-way experiments to gain the maximum benefit from them. Rather like pulling a pendulum back before swinging it in the other direction, this experiment allows you to compare two extreme ways of paying attention, and you might want to think about achieving a happy medium in the end, allowing your attention to come and to go more naturally and spontaneously.

Making use of observation: curiosity in practice

If you went to the departures gate at an airport you would see lots of people saying goodbye to each other. At the arrivals gate you would see another lot of people meeting up and greeting each other. As a curious observer of people in this setting you would notice that there are an enormous number of different ways of parting and greeting. What happens depends on many things: the age of the people, how well they know each other, their nationality, their moods, how long they will be, or have been, apart, who else is with them and so on. There is clearly no single way, and therefore no objectively right way, of conducting this common social interchange, even though it is one of the most basic of all.

But shy people, and people who are socially anxious, often talk as if they were in danger of 'doing it wrong' – as if they had a notion of an ideal way to behave. They also assume that what they do will fall short of this ideal, and therefore run the risk of being 'unacceptable'. But whose is the ideal? Looking at widely disparate groups suggests either that ideals are very different between people or that the range of acceptable practice is much wider than anxious people suppose it is. In the end people do whatever they feel comfortable with, or what works for them. Which is why there is no *need* to be self-conscious about the way you do things, at least from other people's point of view.

If there are no absolute ideals for how we should behave, moment by moment, with each other, then there is no reason to suppose that doing something in an unusual way, or in a way that feels wrong, attracts the attention of others. Here are some facts that socially anxious people have found out, through the experiments that they have conducted. If you were able to turn yourself into a scientist again, curious to find out about the social life around you and how it works, you could double-check these findings, and see if they were true for you, and in your circumstances, too.

Some observations made by others

- Usually symptoms of social anxiety feel worse than they look. When you think everyone can see the shaking or nervousness that you can feel, you are usually wrong.
- Even when people do notice, they usually pay little attention, as it does not have much significance for them.
- People often look calm even when they do not feel calm.
- Most people do not notice much about what others do. They are more likely to be preoccupied with their own concerns.
- Most people do not spend much time judging, criticizing or evaluating others.
- Practically no one is completely happy with the way they are, or with the way they manage to get on with others.

One of the odd things about social anxiety is that it produces a number of paradoxical effects. You may feel as if you are the centre of attention at the same time as feeling so inferior and inadequate that you believe that no one is at all interested in you. You may become preoccupied with yourself and with what is happening to you, and susceptible to painful bouts of self-consciousness, but at the same time be quite uncertain about your identity – about who you are. You want to do things right, and to be acceptable, but still want your individuality to be recognized and to be able to realize your potential. You do not want to be disregarded, but yet want to be invisible. You think you are not worth noticing, but are quite sure that everyone notices you. You want to keep the bad feelings in check, but find it hard to stop doing things that make them worse. Some people, noticing these paradoxical effects, can be misled into thinking that being socially anxious is a kind of self-importance; that it is based on the assumption that you matter so much that everyone pays, or should pay, you lots of attention. In fact, social anxiety is more often based on the opposite assumption – that you are in some way weak, inferior, inadequate or less good than others, combined with the fear that this, supposedly inherent, inferiority will be noticed and have dire consequences for your ability to get on with people and to feel that you belong.

A postscript on self-consciousness and keeping safe

When overtaken by a bout of self-consciousness it can be extremely difficult to wrest your attention away from yourself – hence the practical suggestions above to help you do it, and hence the need to practise by first focusing your attention externally in situations that are not too threatening. There is another possibility, also, that might help to explain why it is difficult to put the suggestions in this chapter into effect. This is that the inward focus that goes with self-consciousness, and increases it the longer it continues, can be another way of protecting yourself. It can feel as if you dare not focus your attention on the outside world, for fear of what you might find out there – as if you were fearful of picking up other people's negative signals. This fear makes it hard to turn your attention outwards: to look straight at someone when you know you are about to blush, or think you have made a fool of yourself in some way: to let them see you 'at your worst', and have to watch their reactions when they spot your vulnerability. It is easier to glance briefly up and then look away, retreating into yourself again, than to give up the self-protection altogether. But brief ventures into the outside world in this way tend to increase your fear rather than to reduce it. They alert you to the possibility of danger out there without giving you long enough to assess its reality or to think about how to defuse it.

The self-protective attempts of inward focus are understandable but they fail. They fail to protect you because they curtail your curiosity and make it impossible to confound your fears. So fear of what is out there increases the fear of what might happen next (anticipatory anxiety); it demands your attention in the present moment, and the bad feelings tend to haunt you afterwards. In other words, inward focus affects your *perception* – what you notice, and therefore the information that gets into your mind; it affects the way you *interpret* the information that you have perceived, and influences how you think about it; and it determines the kind of information that you store about what happened, so it also affects what you *remember* afterwards. The ideas in this chapter are mostly about how to change what you notice: how to make sure that you keep in touch with what is really happening and do not deprive yourself of accurate information about the world outside yourself. The theme running through this chapter is that self-consciousness, focusing your attention on to your inner experiences, fills your mind predominantly with information that makes you feel worse.

Of course, this affects your thinking and your behavior as well as your feelings. So the methods for changing patterns of thinking and for doing things differently fit together well with those for reducing self-consciousness. It makes good practical sense, when starting to work at overcoming your shyness and social anxiety, to concentrate on one method at a time. Then you can work out which aspect of the problem to focus on first, or to put most energy into changing, because it causes you most problems. But in the end you will find that the methods fit naturally together, so that thinking differently and reducing negative patterns of thinking help you to do things in different ways, and to become involved, socially, in more spontaneous, less self-conscious, ways. In the next chapter we will expand these ideas, and also focus more on the information that is stored in memory. Although you cannot change your experience – you cannot change what has happened to you – you can use your memory differently, so that you are no longer haunted by past memories and restricted by unnecessary fears. The aim of the next chapter is to explain what you can do to build your confidence.

KEY POINTS

- Self-consciousness comes from focusing your attention inwards.
- It is at the centre of all the vicious cycles that help to keep the problem going.
- It also makes the problem worse.
- Focusing attention inwards fills you with information about yourself and your reactions to feeling anxious. It also means that you have less attention available for things outside yourself. So feeling self-conscious leaves you short of accurate, detailed information. It leaves you with a hazy impression of what was going on.
- Reducing self-consciousness involves: working out how self-consciousness affects you; deciding not to think about unpleasant experiences; filling your mind with something else.
- It is extremely helpful to use your sense of curiosity. Think of yourself as a scientist who is finding out more about social interactions. You could carry out two-way experiments, in easy situations first; and you could turn yourself into an accurate, interested and curious observer.
- It may take some courage to stop retreating into yourself, and instead to focus on what is happening around you. Although the retreat feels safer, it can make you vulnerable to episodes of self-consciousness. Facing the world is a far safer option in the end.
- Self-consciousness influences what you perceive, how you interpret it and what you remember. Broadening your focus of attention changes what you perceive; working on your thoughts can change how you interpret what happens; and doing things in a new way starts to fill your memory with new things, so that the three strategies described so far fit together well.

10

Building up confidence

Everyone who suffers from social anxiety is likely to benefit to some degree from the three strategies described so far: changing thinking patterns, doing things differently and reducing self-consciousness, especially if they do some of the exercises described in Chapters 7, 8 and 9. You may find that making these changes is enough, or you may continue to feel shaky and at risk for considerably longer than you had hoped – as if something could still go wrong for you at any time. If you cope better with your difficulties at times, but still feel unconfident underneath, as if the changes do not rest on a sure foundation, then do not be tempted to give up. Persistence is likely to lead to progress, even when the changes seem too slow and insubstantial to make a noticeable difference at first. The reason for working systematically on building up your confidence as well is that it helps to hasten these changes.

Where does confidence come from?

Many people assume that confidence is something that you either have or do not have, as if it were determined by the fact that you inherited a strong personality, or was written in the stars. But this assumption – whatever it is based on – is false. Another common assumption is that confidence comes from experience; from the things that happened to you and from the way you were treated as you grew up. If, for example, the people around you were encouraging and appreciative, and did what they could to foster your development; if they were not too harsh in their use of criticism and punishment, and built you up rather than undermined you; if you fitted in well at school and were able to make friends – then you should have all that is necessary for being confident. If not, then the opportunity for becoming confident has been missed once and for all, and the foundation is just not there. But this is not true either. As was explained in Chapter 4, many factors combine to make you the way you are. Whatever your age, and whatever your life-story might suggest, your self-confidence can still increase.

BOX 10.1: NON-SOCIAL ACTIVITIES THAT CONTRIBUTE TO CONFIDENCE

- Being able to driving a car, or cook a meal, or plan a holiday.
- Choosing what you like in the way of music, or pictures, or plays; TV shows, or films; books to read; sporting activities; hobbies, e.g. gardening, photography, making a collection.
- Skills: playing a sport, or musical instrument, or making things, or using a computer or word processor.
- Running things: a house, or a club or a business.
- Working skills: organizing yourself, planning your day, managing your time efficiently.
- Keeping your financial or tax affairs in order.
- Using your knowledge: identifying plants, or cars, or antiques; doing crosswords; improving your home.

There are some facts about confidence that it might be useful to know. First, there are many different ways in which someone can be confident, or unconfident. I am confident that I can cook a good meal for a family celebration, but unconfident that I can learn to use the program on my computer for drawing diagrams. A shy or socially anxious person might have no qualms about various demanding or highly sophisticated activities, like climbing a mountain, or being able to understand the chemical composition of a new drug, but still find it difficult to enter a room full of people. So the degree of confidence that you feel is not a fixed quantity, but depends on what you are doing. This means that you should beware of thinking of yourself as unconfident *as a person*, and instead try to divide your confidence up into its component parts. Some examples of the many, non-social, activities that contribute to feeling confident are listed in Box 10.1.

Is self-confidence different from this?

This is a difficult question to answer. People who are not self-confident talk as if they have a general lack of confidence, and they can describe some of the ways in which this affects them. These include such things as being tentative in the way they approach things; being reluctant to try anything new or to show initiative; being more prone to uncertainty and to doubt before, during or after doing something they find difficult; and wanting to seek reassurance from others, and to keep their perceived weaknesses well hidden. It is as if their lack of self-confidence makes them feel inadequate or inferior or incompetent compared to the people around them, and as if others do not have similar doubts; as if lacking self-confidence sets them apart from other people, and makes them different.

But even for people who say they have no self-confidence at all, there are some things that they feel confident about. One difference between them and others is that they undervalue, ignore or discount these things, as if they were not important and had no significance. So they might be able to map read, or keep small children amused for an afternoon, or keep their potted plants alive throughout the winter, or install a new computer program; but such things do not weigh with them. They discount them as if they had no personal meaning, and assume that their kind of 'unconfidence' is somehow more fundamental than this. Having compared themselves with others, they draw conclusions in terms of what this means about them 'as a person', and then assume that their presumed defects matter more than other, less socially relevant, abilities, such as being good at keeping accounts, or writing letters, or sports.

But confident people also have doubts about themselves. This is because the amount of confidence that self-confident people feel at any particular time is not fixed and constant from moment to moment, even though it may appear to others to be so. So the confidence they feel does not depend only on what they are doing. It depends on other things too, such as their general attitudes about what matters, and their moods; on how they are feeling. At low moments, when feeling dispirited or tired or lacking in energy and initiative, the feeling of confidence may seem to ebb away. Sometimes it springs back as soon as the feeling changes for the better, and sometimes it is slow to return. Anyone's confidence can take a jolt, for instance if they suffer a painful rejection or an apparently endless run of bad luck, or make a mistake that they 'should have been able to foresee'. Confidence ebbs and flows, and this means that everyone, confident people included, sometimes worries about things that normally would hardly bother them – and sometimes with good reason.

As already mentioned, many people – even most people – can look confident even when that is not how they feel. Some consciously adopt a veneer of confidence, and then they can, for example, introduce their partner to a colleague even when they feel nervous. Others may, almost unconsciously perhaps, draw on the assumption that, even if they 'do it badly', it will not really matter. So they might stumble over the words, or make the introduction in a gauche and awkward way, but not let this bother them too much. They can allow it to flow out of the mind like water flows down the river, go on to the next thing without dwelling too much on the temporary embarrassments that happen to everyone.

Behaving 'as if'

When you put on the veneer, then people tend to take you at your own estimation – and assume that you are as confident as you look. This is one reason why socially anxious people often suppose that they are less confident (and less competent) than others. They are aware of what it feels like inside and cannot easily tell how unconfident other people feel. It is also why one of the most useful and helpful strategies to adopt is to behave 'as if' you were more confident than you feel.

Ask yourself, when joining a conversation for instance, or when you are about to enter a room full of people and feel like sliding invisibly through the door, and slipping quietly round behind those who are already there, how you would behave if you really were confident. How would you enter the room then? How would you look? Or move? Or behave? How would you stand? Adopting a confident posture, and being ready to meet other people's gaze, for example, changes the whole situation. It helps you to interact in an apparently more confident way, and then has a remarkable effect on how confident you feel. This is because the behavior and the feelings link up. The link is obvious when you *feel* anxious and *behave* nervously, but less obvious when you *behave* confidently and then *feel* better. So behaving the way you want to feel can bring about the thing you want to happen.

The effect will be even stronger if, knowing that thoughts, feelings and behaviors interact, you add in the link with thoughts, and give yourself an encouraging message or adopt a confident way of thinking as well. Again, if your head is full of self-doubts and self-denigration you will feel bad and your behavior will be less confident. Instead, saying something to yourself that reflects the confidence you do not yet feel, but would like to feel, such as 'It's fine to be the way I am', or 'I'm doing OK', 'I want to be friendly', or 'None of these people are really out to threaten me', may help to bring about the sense of confidence from which the rest follows. Behaving 'as if' this were true can make a big difference to how you feel, to what you do, and also to what happens to you next, as different behavior from you elicits different behavior from others and so on.

Seeking out success

Nothing works so well as success when trying to defeat anxiety, so another valuable way to build confidence is to take part in activities in which 'success', in social terms, is easier to come by, or to think of ways of joining in that oil the wheels of communication once you get there. Researchers have found that people forget themselves and their anxiety more easily if they are involved in activities that are helpful to others. Participating in altruistic activities such as a community project to raise funds for a new playground, or to make access to the local shops easier for disabled people, provides a context in which many people can more easily forget themselves, and it provides a sense of belonging that can help to counteract the socially anxious person's sense of difference or isolation. Working together with others on a joint concern eases communication in many ways, whatever the particular cause: political, social, educational, cultural, sporting or of some other kind. People who doubt their competence, or acceptability, or adequacy, in other situations find that being able to contribute as part of a group helps to remove these doubts. So, if there is some cause that people around you are involved in, or one that is of particular interest to you, then joining in could provide the kind of success experience that gives your confidence a boost.

With the boost behind you, it is often easier to tackle something harder that might feel more personally relevant, like asking someone out for a date or speaking up in front of a group.

Doing things with people you find especially unthreatening provides another helpful context for confidence building. Whom exactly you find unthreatening will depend on you; examples include people younger than yourself, or children, or older people, or single people, or people who have young families, or people who live in a certain neighbourhood, or people who need help in some way, or family members and so on. The principle is a simple one: success breeds success. If you can seek it out, then you will be able to use it to build up your confidence.

Underlying beliefs and assumptions

Confidence grows when things go well for you, and it comes partly from doing things that you find difficult, rather than avoiding them or withdrawing from them. The more you do, the more likely it is that your confidence will grow. However, for some people there are certain underlying beliefs and assumptions that persist despite the changes they make. Then it is useful to focus on changing those underlying beliefs and assumptions as well, and the three strategies described in Chapters 7, 8 and 9, 'Changing Thinking Patterns', 'Doing Things Differently' and 'Reducing Self-Consciousness', provide valuable tools for doing this when combined with the strategies described in this chapter. This is because the different levels of thinking, or cognition, at which they operate fit closely together, and what happens at one level influences what happens at the others.

A reminder about the different levels of cognition

The three levels of thinking distinguished in Chapter 3 were the level of attention, the level of automatic thoughts and the level of underlying beliefs and assumptions (see pages 45–52). The deepest cognitive layer, so to speak, according to this way of dividing thoughts up, is the level of the *beliefs*, which for all of us reflect our basic attitudes: 'I can handle most of the things that come my way'; 'People are usually trustworthy'; 'Things are bound to go wrong some of the time'. As these examples show, one way of dividing up the sorts of beliefs that people have is to think of them in terms of whether they apply to yourself, to other people or to the world in general. *Assumptions* are like rules for living that fit with the underlying beliefs: 'If I was asked to do something new I could probably learn how to do it'; 'If people are friendly towards you, you can mostly believe what they say'; 'If things sometimes go wrong, then it is important to remember that they sometimes go right too'. As these examples show, thinking at any level can be predominantly positive as well as being predominantly negative.

At the next level are *automatic thoughts* that reflect what comes into one's mind, or the continuous, moment-to-moment stream of consciousness, whether or not it has been put into words: 'This is going to be difficult', 'He was really friendly to me', 'This is about to go horribly wrong'.

At the level of *attention* are all the things that people notice and pay attention to: the internal feeling of dread and sense of hesitation, and all the features of self-consciousness that were discussed in the previous chapter, as well as glimpses of other people's smiles and frowns.

These three levels of thinking fit together. Someone who *believed* that other people were mostly hostile, *assumed* he should 'never let his armour drop', *thought* that they were always looking for ways to put him down, *noticed* their failure to smile or say 'good morning' to him. If you *believed*, underneath, that 'People are usually critical and rejecting', then you might *assume* that 'If you meet someone new, you should be wary of them, and keep on your guard'; *think* thoughts such as 'They don't like me', and *notice* your nervousness when faced with strangers. The point of emphasizing this idea here is that when negative beliefs and assumptions predominate over more positive ones, or are especially powerful, they can continue to influence your thinking and what you notice despite your best efforts to change your thinking patterns, your behavior and your self-consciousness. Then they need special attention. Learning how to change your beliefs and assumptions as well will help you to make all the other changes that you would like to make.

Where do beliefs and assumptions come from?

People are not born with their beliefs ready made. These beliefs are more like conclusions that they have come to on the basis of what happens to them. Thinking patterns develop over many years, and when people have had long-standing difficulties such as those that affect their social lives, then they have often drawn more drastic conclusions than others, and have stronger, more dominant, negative beliefs and assumptions than those others. For example, someone who remembered being punished severely and unpredictably as a child came to believe: 'I am always doing things wrong', and developed a rule for living to go with this belief: 'If you keep out of the way, you will also keep out of trouble.' The important point about this is that, in these circumstances, the belief made sense, and the rule for living that went with it served a useful function. This is true even though this person had not put these ways of thinking into words before seeking help.

In this example, the belief and its associated way of thinking helped the person avoid some of the punishment that might otherwise have come his way. But 'keeping out of the way' is not such a useful rule later on in life, when wanting to be able to meet people, make friends, start work, and build up satisfying partnerships and relationships. So 'old' beliefs are sometimes outdated, and one of the aims of the methods described next is to help you to update and revise any of your beliefs that get in the way of change, and to develop new rules for living that work better for you now. When underlying levels of thinking change, then the surface ones become easier to change too.

Often we do not know where the beliefs and assumptions that we have ended up with came from. But sometimes they seem to have developed after particular distressing events, like being teased and rejected at school, being harshly criticized, or feeling humiliated and embarrassed in front of people whose opinion was important.

Such experiences can provide compelling evidence for the beliefs at the time, and leave you with painful memories or images, but they do not prove that the beliefs are generally true. Someone who was teased or bullied at school might well come to hold a belief such as 'I am unacceptable', and this belief could persist until it is brought out into the open and re-examined.

When such beliefs and assumptions prevent you making progress, it is important to learn to step back and take a cool look at them. The aim is to think about them again, as if from a completely different standpoint, and to see them as someone else might see them. Ask yourself whether the belief seemed once to be true, but is now outdated; or whether it is exaggerated. Is anybody *totally* unacceptable, for instance? Is this more like a feeling – based on unpleasant, distressing memories – than a thought based on hard fact? Learning how to change beliefs and assumptions should help you, when answering questions such as these.

How beliefs and assumptions work

Our beliefs and assumptions provide the framework with which we approach the world. It is as if everything that happens to us, everything we see, think and involve ourselves in, has to be sifted through this filter on its way in.

An analogy may be helpful. Imagine that the way in which all of us filter the information that comes to us is like a window on the world. Then the shape of that window, and the colour of the glass in it, and where we stand in relation to it, determine what we see. If the window is too small, or has coloured, dirty or uneven glass in it, then it will limit or distort what we can see. If we could look through another window instead – or come closer so that we could see out properly, or open it wide so that we did not have to peer through the glass – then we would see things differently. All of these actions would give us a new perspective; but most of us do not do these things because we assume that our view of the world is realistic. We do not stop to think about the characteristics of the window we may be looking through, but suppose that our view is the correct, or even the only possible, one.

For example, a friendly invitation to come out for a drink, seen through the eyes of someone who believed that nobody liked him, provoked these comments: 'She must have been pushed for company'; 'She probably just felt sorry for me'; 'Maybe she wants me to do something for her'; and later he added, 'Nobody wants me around' – as if the invitation had in fact never happened. He had, in fact completely forgotten about it by the time he was prompted to talk about it a few days later. From his perspective, the friendliness of the invitation was not even part of the picture.

Changing underlying – or undermining – beliefs

Underlying beliefs reflect what things mean to you. They often 'go without saying', and they may be hard to put into the exact words that fit for you, partly because meanings are sometimes elusive. They also seem obviously true when you believe them, so that there seems to be no point in questioning them. But this is wrong, as beliefs can be just as false, misguided, unhelpful or outdated as any other kinds of thoughts.

Some examples of the beliefs of other socially anxious people may help you to identify the kinds of beliefs that undermine your confidence. Remember, as described in Chapter 3, these beliefs may be more like an underlying sense of yourself than a clear statement that you regularly put into words, and they tend to reflect categorical judgments – or judgments that are supposedly absolutely right or wrong and admit of no half-measures, such as 'I am odd ... weird ... different ... boring ... unattractive', or 'I am inferior ... inadequate ... unacceptable ... unlikeable'. They reflect your ideas and impressions about how other people are too: 'Other people are always judging you ... criticizing ... never unconfident or anxious'; or 'Others don't like people who are nervous ... shy ... quiet' (see page 51). These beliefs often sound – and may feel – like statements of fact, although in reality they reflect opinions and attitudes rather than facts, and therefore can be questioned, re-examined and rephrased, perhaps in less categorical, or absolute, terms. Two straightforward steps for helping you do this are described next.

Step 1: Identifying your own personal beliefs

Start by thinking of a recent situation in which you felt socially anxious: a situation in which your individual version of the problem caused you distress or difficulty. It is best to have a particular situation in mind (like 'going to Jenny's house last week'), rather than a *type* of situation (like 'meeting new people'). Good examples would be situations like a time when you got angry with someone but could not say so, or a time when you heard the voices of people talking in the room you were about to enter and stopped because you were suddenly flooded with feelings of anxiety and dread. Then you should think through this situation from beginning to end, without avoiding anything about it that might make you shudder again in retrospect, or make you feel reluctant to face up to its full implications.

Identifying beliefs and assumptions can be a painful business, so give yourself time and try not to rush into it. Remember that many other people have similar beliefs. You are not the only one who has to work at them in order to feel better, and do the things that you want to do. Make yourself go through all the details of what happened by describing them to yourself, or by talking yourself through it again, or by imagining that you can see it all on an internal video screen. Pay attention to the thoughts, the general impressions and the images that come to mind, and to any internal monologue or dialogue with yourself that was going on at the time. Focus on what you think you did 'wrong' in that situation. Then ask yourself the following key questions:

Key questions for identifying beliefs

- What do you think were your shortcomings?
- How are you judging yourself?
- What did it mean to you, that it was so problematic?
- What does it mean about you?
- What are the attitudes of others?
- What does this tell you about them?

The aim is to clarify what the situation meant to you then, and what it still means to you – and about you – now. Then, with one of your 'social failures' fully in mind, complete each of these sentences:

1 I am ....

2 Others are ....

Use whatever words come to mind to express your inner beliefs. Your own words will reflect the particular shade of meaning that is important to you, so although many people may have the same kinds of beliefs, for example about not being likeable, or acceptable, or attractive, they will express them in different ways, and these slight differences reflect their different personalities and experiences.

You could broaden your understanding of yourself and your underlying beliefs by thinking through other difficult or embarrassing events that have happened to you as well. You may find that you always come to the same conclusions, or you may find that you have a relatively large set of beliefs, and that different ones come to the fore at different times. If so, ask yourself whether one of the beliefs is more important or more fundamental to you than the others. More fundamental beliefs, or *core beliefs*, tend to be ones that arouse the strongest feelings, and are most closely related to your worries and fears. They are the ones that make you want to protect yourself most, and to seek out ways of keeping yourself safe, as facing up to them and to their implications is especially painful. Nobody wants to come to the considered conclusion that 'nobody likes me', for instance, and this is harder if the conclusion reflects an even more fundamental judgment about yourself, such as: 'I'm not the sort of person people can like.'

At this stage it is important to remember that categorical beliefs such as this are extremist statements (see page 149), and likely to be wrong, and they are also changeable; but you cannot change them without knowing what they are. If identifying the belief makes you feel worse, or much worse, try to console yourself with the thought that the bad feelings will not last, and the worse you feel the more likely it is that you have succeeded in identifying the crucial beliefs for you. *That does not make the beliefs true*: it just makes it more important that you learn how to re-examine, and modify them.

Step 2: Changing beliefs

The second step, just as when changing other kinds of thinking patterns (see Chapter 7), is to re-examine these beliefs, and to separate the facts from the opinions. However true they seem at first, such categorical beliefs are very likely to be exaggerations or over-generalizations, and they should certainly be questioned. Here are some more key questions to ask yourself:

Key questions for changing beliefs

- Would you judge someone else who felt like you do in the same way? What would you say to someone else who held a belief like this one?

- Are you being fair to yourself?
- Are you going in for 'character assassination', rather than sticking to what happened on one particular occasion?
- Are you forgetting that everyone makes mistakes, gets things wrong, and feels socially uncomfortable at times? That no one can be perfect?
- Are you ignoring your strengths and focusing on your weaknesses? Ignoring the successes and friendships, while focusing on failures and embarrassments?
- Are you falling into a biased pattern of thinking? Catastrophizing? Taking things personally? Mind reading? Emotional reasoning? (See the list on page 140.)
- Are you drawing conclusions on the basis of your childhood or adolescent experiences?
- Are you judging yourself as you have (once) been judged? If so, what makes the person, or people, who judged you right now? Who is the best authority on you? Other people or yourself?

The easiest way to start this work is to use one of the thought records that were described in Chapter 7. The blank versions of these forms and the key questions for copying are in the Appendix. Write your belief down in the column for upsetting thoughts, and then work through the form in the way that was explained in Chapter 7.

Questioning underlying beliefs can occasionally have dramatic effects. This happens when it is immediately obvious that the 'old' belief is so exaggerated or so extreme or so outdated that it must be false. For example, Simon, who was bullied and tormented while he was at school, and had subsequently done his best to keep out of sight and therefore out of mind, realized when answering these questions that one of his basic beliefs was 'Everyone out there wants to pick on me'. As soon as he started to question this belief he realized that, although it had seemed true once, it was (now) false. No one had really picked on him for years. But the fear that they might do so was still there, and because the belief had not been brought out into broad daylight and given proper consideration it was still affecting his behavior. In this case Simon's negative thinking pattern – the undermining belief – started to change quickly, and the change was consolidated because Simon also started doing things differently.

The next thing Simon did was decide to change all the ways, large and small, in which he had learned to keep himself out of sight – and this was hard work. The behavior patterns that went with the belief that people would always pick on him were second nature by the time he had left school, so that as an adult he hardly noticed when they occurred. For example, he never – if he could help it – made a suggestion or asked anyone a question; and he was used to positioning himself behind other people, in the least conspicuous place he could find. He had been doing these things so long that he was no longer consciously aware of doing them. So although it was relatively easy for him to recognize that the belief was now false, changing still took time and effort, and it involved doing things differently – including choosing different, more colourful clothes to wear – as well as changing his (outdated) patterns of thinking. So working at changing behaviors is important when working on beliefs; otherwise old habits persist, and contribute to maintaining the difficulties.

As might be expected, at times Simon found that doing things in a new way – 'as if' most people would accept him in the normal way – filled him with fear and dread. This is understandable too. Anyone would feel fearful if they did something they truly believed was risky and threatening. This is the social equivalent of putting your head in the lion's mouth, and it makes feeling anxious about behaving in a new way almost inevitable. But it does not mean that you cannot change, or that trying to change is bad for you and could make you worse. It just means that confronting an old fear brings the fear out into the open, and this is not pleasant. More ideas about how to do this follow, but first it is worth saying something about how knowing what your beliefs are, and being able to use this knowledge, helps you to make lasting change.

Socially anxious people are not cowards or wimps, and they have all faced their fears and suffered their symptoms repeatedly by the time they seek help. Their fear and anxiety are real and disturbing, but somehow facing up to the fears, and doing things that they find threatening, have not changed the problem. Some of the vicious cycles that keep the problem going have already been described, but there is another reason why their courage so far has not succeeded in changing their expectations, and this is that they did not know how to use this courage to change their underlying beliefs. So when things go well for them they tend to react as if they have 'got away with it', or had a lucky escape, and not as if they have learned anything new. In order to change expectations it helps to understand more precisely what the expectations are based upon – to understand the beliefs as well. Then the courage involved in doing new or difficult things is more likely to be rewarded, as old patterns of thinking change too.

The example of Simon might suggest that learning to question your beliefs is easy. But often it is not. This example has been chosen for two reasons: first, to show that it can be done, and secondly because many people know 'at some level' that their undermining beliefs are not really true, even though they *feel as if* they are. So they might feel inadequate even while knowing in their rational minds that they are not. This is an example of emotional reasoning, and this type of negative thinking pattern is particularly common when long-standing beliefs are undermining your confidence. The first line of defence against it has already been described in Chapter 7, 'Changing Thinking Patterns': it is to start rethinking the beliefs, and distinguishing the thoughts from the feelings, by working through a few of your difficult situations using the 'thought records' described earlier.

It is harder to change the framework with which you approach the world, and to rethink your beliefs, than to re-examine the kinds of negative patterns of thinking described so far. It can take a lot longer to convince yourself that it makes sense to change your mind when your belief has shaped your social sense of yourself for a long time. If you truly believe that you are different or peculiar, and that this makes you unacceptable or inadequate, then it is difficult to see things another way, and everything you do seems at first to fit with the old belief. So the rest of this chapter describes some more ways of working on stubborn, long-lasting and undermining beliefs.

Searching for new information

The first of these involves starting a search for new information: information that contradicts, or does not fit with, your belief, using the 'counter-belief worksheet' shown below in Boxes 10.2 and 10.3. A blank copy of this form for you to copy is provided in the Appendix with the other worksheets.

The reason for developing this worksheet is that all of us habitually look out for, notice and remember information that fits with our beliefs, rather than that which does *not* fit with our beliefs. If I think I am no good at making pastry, then what I notice each time Christmas comes round and I have to make the mince pies again is that I cannot remember how to do it without looking it up in a book, that I bother about whether I am doing it right, and that the end result is never quite up to scratch (and often more like cardboard than pastry). If you think that you stick out like a sore thumb (and that this will make people pick on you) then, similarly, you tend to keep on the lookout for danger signs, and to notice when other people look at you, or when someone turns a questioning, or supposedly threatening, gaze in your direction.

To start this search, work through some counter-belief worksheets, as in the examples provided in Boxes 10.2 and 10.3. Two examples have been provided here because it is often easier to see when someone else's framework for approaching the world needs to be modified than to see that one's own framework should be, so the first example has no (or little) social relevance, and the line of argument in it should be quite obvious. The second focuses on a relatively common socially anxious belief, and might be harder to follow for people who share this belief.

The steps to go through are these. First write down your belief on the line at the top. Then rate how much you believe this now (0–100 per cent). Think of yourself as doing a forward search, into the future, rather than a backward search into past situations, as this makes it easier to pick up new information than it would be if you relied only on your memory. So think ahead to a situation that you feel anxious or worried about that is relevant to this belief and write it down. Then make your prediction. Ask yourself, on the basis of your belief, what do you think will happen? This is like defining the framework provided by your negative thinking pattern. It is like identifying your expectation, or prediction.

Next, you should define your search plan: what to look out for, so as to step outside this framework. As you can work out from the examples, this is easier to do if you have made a clear prediction first. These three parts of the worksheet should be completed before you enter the situation in question; the next two, concerning the outcome of your search and your conclusions, can only be filled in after the event.

When the event is over, think about what happened, and how that fitted with your expectations and predictions. Summarize your findings, and write down what the search has revealed (the 'adequate' or 'passable' pastry, instead of the tasteless cardboard). Finally, think about the whole exercise, and draw your own conclusions. Try to step outside your usual framework sufficiently to be able to see things afresh. Some key questions you could ask yourself are:

- Has it alerted you to things that you might not otherwise have noticed?
- Has it demonstrated to you how this belief keeps your thinking stuck in a particular pattern?
- Has it disconfirmed any of your predictions or expectations?

The last step in this exercise is to think back to your original belief. There are two kinds of changes that you are looking for. First, rate the degree to which you believe it now on the same (0–100) percentage scale. Secondly, ask yourself if you would like to modify your original belief in any way. Useful modifications would make your belief less extreme, or less negative.

The more new information you find, the more likely it is that your belief rating will start to shift, as your search weakens that belief's hold on you, but this may take some time. If you have held the belief in question for some years, and have focused more on the things that support it than on the ones that discredit it, then the exercise will be difficult. It is hard to start seeing things in a new way, without the old, familiar framework.

If you can adopt the state of mind that this worksheet encapsulates, and keep up the search for new information, then belief change will follow by degrees. One person reacted to doing this exercise with the comment: 'I've been thinking like this so long, that I did not even realize that it could be questioned'.

BOX 10.2: COUNTER-BELIEF WORKSHEET 1

Belief: I'm no good as a cook
How much do you believe this (0–100 per cent)? 80 per cent

The Forward Search Plan

BEFORE THE EVENT
1 *Think of a future situation that will be difficult for you*
My husband's birthday, when I will have to make him a birthday cake and all the family will be there.
2 *Your expectation or prediction (this should fit with your belief)*
I will not be able to remember how to do it, and will spend hours finding a recipe. I will get in a horrible mess in the kitchen, and something is bound to go wrong. It will fall flat, or be heavy and sticky. Or it will be dry and hard. No one will want to eat it and most of it will be left over.
3 *Search plan: What should you be looking out for?*
Things I do remember how to do. Being quick to find a recipe.

The amount of mess, and the amount of time it takes. What the cake turns out like. How much gets eaten.

AFTER THE EVENT
4 *Outcome: What actually happened?*
Much better than I expected. Found a recipe OK. Did make a horrible mess, but it looked good enough. Also most of them ate it and my daughter said it was good. Someone left a lot but my husband asked for some more the next day.
5 *What conclusions can you draw from that?*
It's far less clear than I thought it would be: good and bad bits mixed up. Probably overall not as bad as I predicted, and it tells me I would find it a lot easier if I only did that kind of thing more often.

Rethinking your original belief
How much do you believe it now (0–100 per cent)? 40 per cent (At least I could learn how!)
How would you like to modify your belief, now? I'm not a very good cook . . . yet.

BOX 10.3: COUNTER-BELIEF WORKSHEET 2

Belief: I am not acceptable as I am
How much do you believe this (0–100 per cent)? 65 per cent

The Forward Search Plan

BEFORE THE EVENT
1 *Think of a future situation that will be difficult for you*
Having to meet some of my parents' friends at the weekend.

2 *Your expectation or prediction (this should fit with your belief)*
I will go quiet. I hate small talk, and I can't do it, so there won't
be anything to say. I shall feel that I have let them down.
3 *Search plan: What should you be looking out for?*
Whether other people go quiet too sometimes. Moments when
I do have something to say. The kinds of things people talk about.
How my parents react to having me there. Whether they say
anything that suggests they are disappointed in me.

AFTER THE EVENT
4 *Outcome: What actually happened?*
I felt awful at first, and could only say standard things. But one
person asked me about work, and then there was more to say.
There were a few moments when everyone was quiet. It certainly
wasn't just my fault. Mum is worried about me, being on my
own so much. But she was happy about how the event went,
so I can't have spoiled it for her.
5 *What conclusions can you draw from that?*
Saying the 'standard' things did start me off, in the end, and
then we got out of the small talk quite quickly. I was lucky that
someone asked me about work. I'm certainly not the only one
who goes quiet at times. I am probably more worried about
letting my parents down than they are. They just want me to be
happier.

Rethinking your original belief
How much do you believe it now (0–100 per cent)? 50 per
cent
How would you like to modify your belief, now? It's not acceptable to me to be so anxious, and so much on my own, but being
that way doesn't make me unacceptable – at least to my parents
and their friends.

Building more positive beliefs

Carrying out a search for new information will help you to modify negative, underlying beliefs, and it can also help you to construct the firm foundation from which your confidence can continue to grow. Searching for new ways of looking at things, as you remove the old framework, also helps you to build more positive beliefs.

Positive beliefs, if they are to be most helpful to you, should be phrased in moderate terms, and each person has to work out for themselves what kinds of positive beliefs are likely to work for them. One person settled for the statement: 'I'm a mixture of good, bad and indifferent, much like everyone else.' Another person said to themselves: 'I'm OK as I am. It's OK to be me.' So try to find the words in which you would like to encapsulate a more positive belief for yourself. You should be looking for a belief that helps you to work against the old, negative way of thinking, and that fits with reality, and this means avoiding extremist terms. It is probably not true for any of us that we are wholly and completely lovable, attractive, acceptable, adequate and so on, even though people who love us may accept us totally. Loving and accepting people, when you truly know them, more often means loving and accepting them 'warts and all' – which in turn means that letting people know you 'warts and all' is just letting them know you. It is not letting them 'see through you', or discover your hidden faults and weaknesses in a way that leads inevitably to the end of the relationship.

Use your notebook here, to try out new, positive beliefs. Write one down on the top of a new page, and every day collect some new information that fits with it. Remember this may be out of sight at first. Keep searching, and it will come into view.

Changing assumptions

Beliefs reflect categorical judgments: 'I am useless'; 'People are always judging you'. Assumptions are like rules for living that are based on beliefs, and they are often expressed using words like 'should', 'must', 'ought', 'have to'. However, when it comes to changing assumptions, it is most useful to put them into words as 'if . . . then . . .' statements. Beliefs and assumptions can both be either helpful or unhelpful. An example of an unhelpful assumption frequently made by people who are socially anxious is: 'If people knew what I was really like, then they would reject me.' Such assumptions get in the way of recovery because they affect your behavior – they determine what you do, such as try to be different and to hide your 'real self'. Another common assumption is: 'If others want to know me they'll let me know.' Someone who lives by this rule is unlikely to take the initiative in contacting people or making new friends. The only way to find out if the assumption is incorrect – or indeed correct – is to start taking the initiative. So changing assumptions involves doing things differently:

- What assumptions do you make about yourself?
- What assumptions do you make about others?
- And about who is responsible for the success or failure of your social encounters?

See if you can identify some of the assumptions you make, expressing them as 'if ... then ...' statements. Do you assume that *if* something goes wrong, *then* it must be your fault?

Identifying your assumptions will tell you how to try to change your behavior, as the new behavior should remove the disadvantages of the old, socially phobic behavior. It involves taking a risk, and will certainly not feel safe at first, but it provides another way of challenging the underlying belief that you need to keep yourself safe from potential harm. Once you truly realize that protective behaviors of all kinds, including those that are closely related to underlying beliefs and assumptions, do not really work, then you will find that you can let them go, and 'be yourself'. Realizing that 'it's all right to be the way I am' is one of the keys to becoming more self-confident.

Someone who believed he was likely to be rejected took great care to hide from others what he was really like, and said very little, but this undermined his confidence as he became increasingly isolated and lonely. It follows that one of the most effective ways of changing your assumptions is to change your behavior. Only if you experiment with doing things differently, and try a new behavior, such as letting people know what you are really like, will you be able to find out if the assumption is correct. For example:

Assumption: 'If you disagree with people they will never accept you.'

Old behavior: Always agree. Keep your opinions to yourself.

New behavior: Try saying what you think.
Evaluation: Find out what happens when you do (carry out a search for new information).

After doing something differently, take a moment to think about it. Some of the possibilities in this case might be that you find yourself engaged in an easier kind of conversation, or that saying what you think leads to an interesting discussion. Or you might feel that you are able to make a better kind of contact with people, or even that they react to you differently, for example in a more interested or friendlier way. A summary of the stages to go through when working to change assumptions is shown in Box 10.4.

Many assumptions can be phrased in two ways: either in terms of what you should do, or in terms of what you should not do. For example, if you assume, or live by the rule that saying what you think will lead to conflict, this could be worded either in this way: 'If I say what I think then there will be an argument', or in this way: 'I will get on better with people if I never disagree with them.' Re-examining this assumption follows the same principles, whichever form it takes, and doing so can have many different consequences. It could reveal that the fear of conflict had led to exaggerating the dangers of disagreements, or that the ability to handle conflict, or to handle the strong feelings when conflict arises, had been over-estimated. Obeying rules for living such as this one means that disagreements and conflicts are avoided, and this deprives people of experiences that could be helpful. In the end confidence is more likely to come from accepting that

BOX 10.4: SUMMARY OF STAGES FOR CHANGING ASSUMPTIONS

1 *Identify your assumption*. Think of this as a 'rule for living', that fits with your beliefs. It might first be expressed in words like 'should', 'must', 'ought'. Write it down as an 'if . . . then . . .' statement before going any further.

2 *Identify the behavior that fits with the assumption*. This is the 'old behavior' that reflects how you put the rule for living into practice. Ask yourself, what does this assumption or rule make me do? How do I behave so that I do not break this rule?

3 *Do something differently*. Choose a new behavior that allows you to break the old rule, and to rethink your assumption. You could do this in an easy way first, and build up to harder ways later.

4 *Evaluate what happens*. Try to step outside your old frame-work once again. Think about how things went, about what it means about you that you could choose a new way of behaving, and about what it would mean to you if you could go on like this until you felt more confident.

NB: You may feel anxious when you do this, at first. Try to hang in there when you do, so that you can build your confidence.

disagreement and conflict are inevitable, facing up to them when they occur, and learning how to handle them when they do. (If this is a particular difficulty for you, you may find the ideas summarized in Chapter 12 helpful.)

It is true that expressing opinions may reveal differences between people, but avoiding the expression of these differences, or protecting oneself from having to face them, makes them seem worse than they otherwise would. It is the beliefs and assumptions that make it seem best to avoid 'disasters' and to protect yourself from risks. Changing the beliefs and assumptions helps to de-catastrophize such unpleasantness.

A flashcard, to help you remember the main points

This is a long chapter, and it could be useful to make yourself a flashcard (see page 157) as a reminder of the main points. Flashcards are especially helpful when trying to remember new ways of thinking. On one side of the card you should write a belief or assumption. On the other you should summarize new ways of thinking. You could include reminders of any of the confidence building ideas that have come from reading this chapter, any new information that comes from your searches, or from doing things differently, or any ideas or images that came to mind as you read and that you would like to remember. One person drew some windows on the back of a flashcard, to remind herself about the different perspectives that can come from different places, and from looking through different kinds of glass. What this meant to her was: 'Maybe I have been wrong, in my beliefs. Maybe there is another way of seeing things. Maybe it is worth going on looking, and trying out doing things differently.' A complicated message can be summarized in a few brief symbols. The following key points may also be helpful.

KEY POINTS

- Confidence is not one thing, but many. It develops from experience, and it comes and goes. Even confident people sometimes feel unconfident.
- You can build confidence by behaving 'as if' you were confident, and by seeking out successes.
- Underlying beliefs and assumptions can undermine confidence. They provide the framework within which you see the world, or the window through which you view it.
- They developed during a lifetime of experience, and they can be changed.
- There are two main steps for changing beliefs: first you need to identify them, so that you know what they are; then you need to re-examine them.
- To do this, you will need to step outside the old framework, and search for new information.
- Building up more positive, helpful beliefs also gives your confidence a surer foundation.
- So does changing the assumptions that go with your beliefs. This involves changing old patterns of behavior as well as old patterns of thinking.

11

Putting it all together

You are unlikely to have read this book unless you have suffered from shyness or social anxiety for some time, and when a problem persists it is hard to see where to begin when you want to change it. If you would like to use some of the ideas you have read about so far, then you have already made a step in the right direction. If not, stop and think for a minute. What are your doubts and reservations? Does it all sound too complicated? Do you wonder if you could ever do any of the things described? Do you think that people who can use these ideas probably have a relatively mild problem, and that yours is too deep-seated to respond to the suggestions made here? These sorts of thoughts are common, and if this is what you think, then you probably feel discouraged too, and find it hard to imagine things being any different.

If so, remember that there may be another way of seeing things. The methods for dealing with patterns of thinking described as the first strategy for overcoming social anxiety can be used to examine thoughts about being able to change as well as other kinds of thoughts. Try them and see what you think then. How would you find out if you could over-come your wish to keep yourself safe? Or whether you could divert your attention away from your sense of embar-rassment and distress when you feel self-conscious? Probably only by 'trying and seeing'. This chapter provides some ideas that are intended to make this easier to do. It aims to help you work out how to get the most out of helping yourself, and it starts with a summary.

Summary of strategies for overcoming social anxiety

All the methods described here are intended to help you to break the vicious cycles that otherwise keep the problem going. Although the methods can be simply described, they are not 'simplistic', or superficial. They are based on a sophisticated way of understanding the problem, and they all take some time to learn. You have to learn what to do before you can use them effectively. So do not expect the problem to vanish overnight, and remember that social anxiety is a normal part of life. Most people would feel anxious if they were going for an interview, or if they were publicly criticized, or unexpectedly asked to speak at an important meeting or at a friend's wedding. Nothing you can do will get rid of all social anxiety. But you can learn to overcome the anxiety that interferes with your life, or restricts you, and to keep that anxiety within manageable bounds.

- *Changing thinking patterns*. This method is designed to help you to recognize and to re-examine the way you think. It comes first because the fear in social anxiety focuses on ideas about what other people think about you; on the fear that you will be 'found wanting', or be 'found out'.
- *Doing things differently*. Fear makes you want to keep safe, but safety behaviors and avoidance make the problem worse, not better. Although it feels risky, it is better to stop trying to protect yourself in these ways, as that is the best way to learn that you do not need to do it.
- *Reducing self-consciousness*. Self-consciousness comes from focusing your attention onto yourself. This makes you increasingly aware of uncomfortable sensations, feelings, thoughts and behaviors. Consciously focusing on people and things outside yourself instead allows the distress to die away and keeps you more in touch with what is happening around you.
- *Building up confidence*. Confidence may grow quickly, or it may change more slowly. When it is slow to change this may be because you need also to work on your underlying beliefs and assumptions. You can use the strategies already described to help you to do this, together with some others which help you to step outside your old framework for seeing the world, and search for information that helps you to build a new one.

In order to make the most of your efforts to change, and to keep track of progress, you should get a notebook for your social anxiety work, and use it regularly, even when things are going well and you no longer think it is necessary. Occasional notes made at such times are invaluable when you later have a setback, if you can use them to remind yourself of the changes that you made, and how you were able to make them. Otherwise you may be tempted to think that the improvement was illusory, and that when things deteriorate again that you have just reverted to type. A more helpful way of understanding such ups and downs is to recognize that they are inevitable, and happen to everyone. Patterns of thinking tend to reassert themselves, just like other old habits, and the effort to counteract them may have to be repeated from time to time, until they die away or are replaced with new ones.

Making use of the various worksheets provided will also help you to gain more from the ideas in this book than you otherwise would. Everyone has their own, personal and slightly different version of social anxiety or shyness, so you may want to adapt the worksheets and exercises to suit yourself. Nevertheless, it would be sensible not to take too many short cuts with them, especially of the kind that allows you to leave out the bits that you find difficult, or avoid going into situations that make you anxious. Recovery is not possible without experiencing some of the fear and distress that have sent you in search of help. The reward is that, as things change, and your confidence grows, the fear starts to subside.

How do the different strategies fit together?

You might wonder whether it matters which of the strategies for overcoming social anxiety listed above you start with. They have been presented in this order because it is logical. The sequence starts with strategies for changing negative patterns of thinking because thinking plays such a central part in social anxiety (see Chapter 3). Doing things differently comes next, because once people feel fearful they naturally want to protect themselves, and so they take action to do so. But the actions that they take, mostly using safety behaviors and avoidance, prevent them from overthrowing their expectations, and fuel the vicious cycles that keep the problem going. The methods for reducing self-consciousness come next because when doing social things, feeling self-conscious about it adds another layer of difficulty. Strategies for building confidence come last as not everyone needs to learn these methods. Sometimes making other changes is sufficient. It would therefore be sensible to work through the book in this order if that makes sense to you.

But the order is not invariable, and people who start in different places can also benefit. For example, you may find it easier, and more practical, to work at changing your behavior first. This will be most effective if you stop and think about the meaning of the changes you make, so that you do not fall into the habit of discounting them, or dismissing them, when you find that some things were easier than you thought they would be, or find that you are suddenly able to do things that other people take for granted and treat as 'normal'. When anyone makes a deliberate change of this kind, they deserve the credit for doing so, and at least some of the change they achieve must be attributable to the efforts that they make, and to a change of heart in the way that they were approaching their problems.

Another way of starting is to work first on giving up your safety behaviors, and later to focus on your patterns of thinking, when you summarize what happened and what this means. Sometimes, despite what you might have feared, the interactions you become involved in when not trying to keep yourself safe are so much more satisfying that this gives the process of building – or rebuilding – your confidence a good start.

Yet another way is to focus first on the kinds of behavioral changes that enable you to change your assumptions, or the social rules that you tend to live by. Assumptions tell you what you 'should', 'ought' or 'must' do: 'Unless I dress up smartly and wear lots of make-up, people will not find me attractive', or 'You have to be witty and amusing, or people will just ignore you'. Working on these assumptions immediately suggests what these people should do: dress less smartly, wearing less make-up in the first case; stop making the effort to be witty and amusing in the second. Adopting an attitude of curiosity while doing this both makes it easier to do and helps in defining the (usually inhibiting) effects of trying to be something other than what one is.

A theme that runs through all of the methods suggested in this book is that of 'finding out what really happens'. You can conduct experiments, or fill in worksheets, or focus your attention on what is happening around you rather than inside you, but whatever you do it will be most helpful if you think about it afterwards, and ask yourself how it went. What was the outcome? Doing this makes you into a practical scientist, when overcoming your problem, and helps you to find out what works best for you; and it also stops you thinking about yourself all the time. Theoretically, it can, so to speak, give you something else to think about when you feel anxious, and therefore take your mind off yourself. Thinking about yourself is, socially speaking, inhibiting and stultifying. So you should foster the curiosity that is inherent in this way of working, and try not to worry too much about finding a 'right' way of doing things. With this curiosity to the fore, you could begin with any of the methods that seem to you particularly interesting, or likely to be helpful in your particular circumstances.

Some principles to bear in mind

- *Do not throw yourself in at the deep end.* It is sensible to start with taking small risks, and to tackle harder things, which involve a greater degree of risk or threat, once you have built your confidence and know more about how the methods work for you.
- *When you have had one successful experience, do not leave things there, but try the same thing again, as soon as you can.* Consolidate your gains, and remember that the more you do the more likely you will notice a change. Do not give up if this is slow to come at first.

- *Do not work at the problem in fits and starts.* If you do, your progress will follow suit, but your moods and feelings may exaggerate the stops and starts until you feel alternately pleased and cast down, as if you were riding a rollercoaster. Instead, try to keep up a steady push in the right direction, for example for two or three months in the first instance.

- *Be realistic about the things you decide you will try.* Do not decide, in your head or on paper, to do something that in your heart of hearts you know is too difficult, and that you will be most unlikely to be able to do. Success is built upon success, so it does not matter how small the success is that you start with. It may be as small as making fleeting eye contact, or remembering to smile at someone in the morning. If it works, and you repeat it often enough to know that there are occasions when it does not work as well as others, then you will be able to move on faster than if you had started with something that gave you a sense of disappointment or failure.

- *When you have decided which of the strategies to start with, give it a fair trial before you move on to something else.* This is tempting if the strategy does not seem obviously helpful the first few times you try it, or if you get bored with doing similar things rather often. Stick with each one until you are sure you understand how it works for you. That way you are likely to be able to make the most of all of the strategies that you need.

Enlisting the help of other people

Overcoming this kind of problem can be lonely work. You are the only one who knows exactly how you feel, the only one who has to face deciding what to do about the problem, and the only one who can take appropriate action. Many people who are shy or socially anxious deal with the problem on their own either because they do not want to tell others about their difficulties or because they do not know people whom they are able to tell.

Working at it alone can be extremely effective, and if you do that then you will know that when things change you are solely responsible for that change. It can also be helpful, though, to have a friend or supporter who is prepared to help, and if that person has the time to read about the problem, that may help them to help you most effectively. Above all, you need their encouragement. It is more helpful if you tell them what you are trying to do. Then they can ask you if you did it, and they might be able to help you out if you meet with difficulties or get stuck. It is not so helpful if they try to push you harder than you are ready to go, or if you rely on them to come with you when you have to face something difficult, or to provide a 'quick fix' of reassurance at ever-increasing intervals.

Some common difficulties

When anxiety seems to 'come out of the blue'

Sometimes symptoms of anxiety can sweep up unannounced, and reach apparently overwhelming proportions when least expected. People often describe this experience as if the anxiety 'came out of the blue', with nothing to set it off or explain it that they can think of. On careful examination later it usually turns out that there was a link between something that was happening and the symptoms of anxiety, but the link was difficult to find or to understand. It may have been that the link was in the meaning of the situation ('this means total rejection again'), rather than in anything specific that happened. Or it could be that a fleeting image encapsulated the meaning of the situation (an image of being humiliated and laughed at). Or a similarity in the situation with earlier distressing events could be the trigger: the sound of someone's voice, the colour of something they are wearing, the smell of the food cooking and so on.

If this happens to you, think first about what the situation means to you, or meant to you. This may give you sufficient clues to work out the connection. But if you find no connection at all, do not conclude that you are going mad, and losing control of yourself or your feelings. Try to accept that often we are not able to identify and recognize all the possible connections and links that are there. It is more helpful to accept that there are likely to be some that we will not be able to fathom out.

WHEN THERE IS NOTHING YOU CAN DO ABOUT YOUR SYMPTOMS

Sometimes there seems no point in telling yourself that you might not tremble or shake because you know that you will, and you also know that there is nothing you can do to prevent it, much as you wished that there were. You will not be able to find in this book any methods that will guarantee that you will not tremble – or indeed suffer from any of the other symptoms of shyness or social anxiety, such as tripping over your tongue and finding that the words you intended to say have come out wrong. The key to dealing with this difficulty is once again to think in terms of what it means to you when these things happen. If you believe that it means something dire about you, for example that you are inadequate or a useless wreck that no one would want to know, then you may be suffering from the effects of your own, personal (understandable but exaggerated) viewpoint. The *meaning* of the symptoms rather than the *fact* of the symptoms should once again be the target for change, and using the strategies for changing patterns of thinking, for changing beliefs and for building confidence are the methods that are most likely to be helpful.

WHEN PAINFUL MEMORIES PERSIST

Some people feel as if memories of the distressing and painful things that happened earlier in their lives keep returning to haunt them. They may have distinct memories or dreams of particular events that recur, bringing at least some of the original distress with them. It is not easy to lay such memories to rest. However, a few suggestions might be helpful. Researchers have found that if people can communicate about these events and the feelings they had at the time, they start to feel better, even if the communication is about something that happened many years ago and is in writing, or spoken into a tape recorder, rather than made directly to another person. There is something about being able to express oneself that helps to relieve this type of distress.

Another strategy that some people have found works for them is to think about what the painful memory means to them, and to develop a new image in their minds that transforms this meaning, and takes away the pain. The idea is to construct a new image, even if it is an unrealistic one, in which the person's needs at the time that they were most distressed are met in some way. So the meaning of the new image is that they are comforted, or rescued, or helped or supported or accepted in some way, and the symbolism of the imagery represents this transformation of meaning. If you would like to try doing this for yourself, you should think about what it was that you needed, or still need, to relieve you of the distress that you feel, and give your mind free play when it comes to imagining how this might come about. Then when the distressing memories return you can consciously call the new image to mind.

WHEN YOU FIND IT HARD TO STOP THE 'POST MORTEM' THAT CAN FOLLOW AN EPISODE OF DISTRESS

The post mortem makes things worse. It is a way of thinking that brings all the negative biases, attitudes and beliefs into the front of your mind, and uses them to interpret, and even to elaborate upon, the bad side of what actually happened. The longer a post mortem goes on, the worse it makes you feel. It can sometimes seem increasingly convincing, even though it usually involves a gradual shift away from reality. There is nothing useful about it. Despite what some people think, going over in your mind the things that happened, what you said and what other people said, what you both did, the way you looked and felt and so on, does not end in useful conclusions about how to do things better. It provides no valuable clues about how to overcome the problem. Far better to close down the process as soon as you notice it happening, and to distract yourself with something more interesting instead.

WHEN LOW SELF-ESTEEM GETS IN THE WAY

Low self-esteem is different from low self-confidence. It is about your values, and whether you live up to them; it is about your sense that other people value and accept you irrespective of your achievements, and it is about whether you value yourself. When self-esteem is high people feel good about themselves, and when it is low people feel bad about themselves, as if they were 'worthless' or did not count, or had nothing to contribute. Then they become inhibited and hold themselves back, and their ability to contribute shrinks a bit.

Low self-esteem is like a particular kind of belief: a belief about yourself and your value, or worthiness. It can be built up in much the same ways as confidence can be built, and using many of the same strategies. If this is a difficulty for you, then it would be best to focus particular attention on identifying your 'self-beliefs'. Try to give words to your low self-esteem, and then work at changing it in the ways described in the previous chapter.

When you do this, remember that there are no generally accepted yardsticks available for judging the things upon which self-esteem is apparently based. Self-esteem reflects an opinion about you (your own), rather than facts about you, and this opinion may be independent of what other people think. They may think highly of you despite your own (low) self-esteem; or you may feel that they disapprove of you and reject you, and make you feel that you are different and do not belong, and your self-esteem could still be high. You may be wrong about their judgments, and using the ideas in this book will help you to discover that they think far better of you than you suppose; or they may be making a wrong judgment about you, possibly because they do not know you well. If so, as you improve they will have a better chance of discovering their mistake. In either case, it would be a mistake to let other people's opinions, their approval or disapproval, acceptance or rejection, become the measure of your own value.

PART THREE

Some Optional Extras

As the title suggests, the material in this last part of the book has been added because it is often useful but not everyone needs it. Chapter 12 provides a summary of some of the more relevant strategies for becoming more assertive. Chapter 13 explains how the experience of being bullied when growing up can have lasting effects, some of which are similar to the effects of social anxiety, and points the ways towards overcoming these. Chapter 14 is about how to relax, not only as a physical exercise but as part of a plan for developing a more relaxed lifestyle. One thing that these three chapters have in common is that they are all intended to help you to feel more assured, more comfortable and more at ease about being yourself.

The ideas in this third part of the book are explained rather more briefly than those described earlier. This is because it is relatively easy to find other material on these topics elsewhere as well. A list of some of the other books that you might find helpful is provided on page 311.

12

About being assertive

It is easy to understand why people who are shy, or socially anxious, might also find it hard to assert themselves, and to stick up for what they want or what they believe in, especially when confronted with people who may have different priorities or beliefs. Three kinds of fear are obviously linked to unassertiveness: the fear of being judged, or criticized, or evaluated in pejorative terms; the fear of being rejected or excluded; and the fear of being seen through and 'found wanting'. If you are fearful of showing 'weaknesses' then you are unlikely to find it easy to feel that you can meet with others on equal terms, and that makes being assertive difficult. However, some people who find it extremely difficult to be assertive are not socially anxious, and some socially anxious people have few problems being assertive. So although there is an overlap between the two problems they do not always go together, and you should not assume that they do.

Much has been written on assertiveness, and it is now possible to learn about the attitudes and the skills involved by reading about them, watching video material or attending assertiveness training classes. A few of the specific skills that socially anxious people find particularly useful are described in this chapter, and more ideas will be found in the books listed on page 311.

Balancing passivity and aggression

Assertiveness is based on the idea that your needs, wants and feelings are neither more nor less important than those of other people: they are equally important. This means that you are entitled to your own feelings and opinions, and so is everyone else entitled to theirs. The key skills, therefore, are to do with how you put your ideas and feelings across, how you ensure that they are given due consideration, and how you decide how much weight to give to the feelings and opinions of others. Other people may want you to feel and to think differently, and you may want them to do the same, but acting upon these 'wants' puts pressure on you or on others to be different – and that is not fair.

The two main traps into which people fall when they are beset with thoughts and feelings that make them behave in unassertive ways are being too passive and the opposite: being too aggressive. Passivity involves going along with others at some personal cost: for example, always being the non-drinking, car-driving member of the party because other people assume that you will, and not because that is what you have chosen. It involves a loss of control, as might happen if other people made decisions that affected you without due consultation. Passive behavior, carried to its limits, makes you into a doormat, and as the saying goes, 'If you act like a doormat, don't be surprised if people walk on you'. If you do not speak up, then you may end up doing the job that no one wanted to do, but which everyone else was able to refuse.

Of course, there are many reasons why people are aggressive, and many of them have nothing to do with social anxiety, or with being unassertive. However, there is also in some cases an important connection between being – or sounding – aggressive, and being unassertive. For example, if you do not know how to get people to cooperate with you, or fear that they will not do what you want, then one solution is to use threats. Aggressive behavior has various advantages for socially anxious people. It prevents people getting too close, or keeps them at bay, and it can also be a way of cutting discussion short. If you brook no argument, then you will not have to get into a debate. Aggression tends to bring a speedy end to an interaction, and it hides fear or pain. It can feel as if it is more acceptable to be aggressive than to be apprehensive or nervous, as aggressive behavior is more likely to signify strength than weakness in other people's eyes. But the lion – or the lioness – may be more timid than he or she looks.

Neither passivity nor aggression is ultimately satisfactory, both because of the bad feelings they produce in everyone concerned, and because they are unfair. James, who allowed the neighbours to borrow his mowing machine whenever they wished, ended with a large repair bill (and many angry unexpressed thoughts); Susan, who made abrupt, burdensome demands on her staff and her family, ended feeling stressed and alienated instead of supported and efficient, which was her aim; to her it felt as if she alone were responsible for getting everything done, which seemed unfair. But asking for help signified a kind of weakness that threatened her social acceptability: hence her dilemma.

Some people veer between bouts of passivity and bouts of aggression, or find that they burst out of periods of passivity as if propelled by an explosive device. Some people who are passive at home are aggressive at work. So you may recognize both patterns in yourself, and this introduces one of the main themes of this chapter: the theme of balance. It is often difficult, especially when feelings run high, and when opinions differ, to find the middle ground on which to stand up for yourself in a way that does not also put others down. The essence of assertiveness is learning how to do this, and the attitude of fairness: fairness to yourself, as well as fairness to others, is what makes it possible.

Both passive and aggressive reactions to situations lead to 'stuck positions'. Passive people feel that they have no control over the situation, or that they are lacking in social power, while aggressive people feel the opposite: that it is essential to be in control, and to have the power in their own hands. Assertiveness leads the way out of this impasse by helping people to be more flexible, so that they can adapt to each other, and feel less at risk of either extreme. Assertive people neither feel controlled nor have the need to control others. Control is altogether less of an issue for them – which is not to say that they do not want their own way as much as everyone else.

Changing yourself, not others

It seems only natural to want to change other people, especially when you feel that you have been treated unfairly, or dealt an unfair hand. When social anxiety or shyness get in the way, and prevent you standing up for yourself, other people may indeed give you less consideration than they should. Or they may, unfairly, take advantage of you, so that you feel angry, frustrated and resentful. There are many reasons socially anxious people may have for wanting to change other people. The difficulty is that the only person you can change is yourself, and it is surprisingly easy to lose sight of this truism. If you want people to be different – for example, more friendly, or more considerate of your feelings – then how do you achieve your aim? The only way to do so would be to change yourself: to find ways of making yourself more open to friendship, and ways of expressing your feelings so that others take more notice of them.

Social interactions have been likened to a dance, and the analogy can be extremely useful. The steps of one person are matched by those of others. If you change your steps, then those moving with you will be prompted to change theirs too. The changes you make will precipitate changes in them, so that you can adapt to each other (and vice versa, of course). If you know how you want to change, then it will be easier to think about how to change your steps in the dance, and the examples of assertiveness skills provided in the rest of this chapter illustrate how applying the principle of fairness, when you know what you want to achieve, can help you to build your social confidence as well as your assertiveness.

Having the confidence to say 'no'

Often people who lack social confidence find themselves agreeing to things that they wish they had not agreed to. Sometimes they do this because they feel pressured, and give in to others against their better judgment; sometimes they do it in order not to offend or displease the person who asked them; and sometimes it happens because they want to please someone else – for good reasons (wanting to help out a friend) or for less good ones (fear of disapproval). There are probably other reasons too. When you want to say 'no', but feel tempted to say 'yes', then first you should clarify your priorities, secondly you should learn the skills of saying no with assurance, and thirdly, you should be willing to give yourself thinking time.

Clarifying priorities

First, decide what you want. Do you, or do you not, want to do as asked? Here are some examples to bear in mind while thinking through this section:

- look after someone's house plants when they are on holiday;
- take on an extra commitment to relieve someone else, like your boss or someone in your family;
- tidy the house when visitors are expected;
- make all the practical arrangements for a joint family holiday.

If you can, think of an example from your own experience, and with that in mind, think of the cost to you. Think of the time involved. Think of your preferences. Be fair to yourself, and include your likes and dislikes. Being fair to yourself is not being selfish, but giving yourself as much consideration as you would give to others. Of course, if you really want to say 'yes', then you will be able to do so without later feeling you have been put upon, or exploited, or taken advantage of. So can you anticipate what you will feel later?

It is only too easy to say 'yes' for the wrong reasons: for example, to gain approval from the person who asked you, or to get them off your back, or because you cannot find an 'acceptable' way of saying 'no', or to make up for one of your 'perceived' shortcomings. When you say 'yes' you should, theoretically, be agreeing to something which, given all your priorities, you truly want to agree to. What you agree to should be more important to you than what you have to give up in order to do it – and there is always something that you would be doing instead, even if that is taking the time you need to rest and relax and take stock. If you are being fair to yourself, then saying 'no' is not being rude, or uncaring, or uncooperative, or in some other way 'bad', but treating your own needs and wishes as equally important as those of others.

This is where the 'shoulds' come in: 'shouldn't' we all go out of our way to help others? Is it not selfish to do what one wants when one could be accommodating to others? This is an important idea, but not one that detracts from the points made about being assertive. If you believe that you should help in the way asked then, at some level, you will want to give that help. You may be reluctant, and busy, or overburdened, or irritated to be asked, but the principle that you believe in – provided you really believe in it – will help you along. However, this is not the only principle that could be involved. Not every request, or expectation, or demand, is one that you 'should' comply with.

Saying 'no' with assurance

If someone asks you to do something that you truly do not wish to do, then all you need to do is to say no. You are under no obligation to explain yourself. You have as much right to say no and to leave it at that as the next person. However, many people fear that saying no will provoke further difficulties for them, such as pressure, confrontation, disapproval or even rejection, and they find it easier to say no if they know how to ensure that others will accept their decision. One way to do this is to find as many ways of expressing your decision as you can, and to repeat them calmly and simply, without adding in additional reasons. Saying too much when you want to say no can make you sound overly apologetic, or as if you are making excuses. For understandable reasons, this is known as the 'broken record' technique: 'No, I am sorry but I can't.' 'No, not this time.' 'No, I'm afraid not.'

It does not always work, partly because some people make it hard for us by refusing to take 'no' for an answer. Strategies for saying no with sufficient assurance to convince others that you mean it can therefore contribute to your sense of fair play. Here are some of the ways of making a refusal easier for someone else to accept, and easier for you to give.

- Make it clear that you appreciate being asked: 'Thanks for asking'; 'I appreciate you thinking of me.'
- Acknowledge the other person's priorities and wishes: 'I know it is important to you'; 'I understand the difficulty.'
- Give a clear reason for your refusal: 'I have to . . . visit my grandmother . . . complete my tax return . . . plan next week's work.'
- Help the other person to solve the problem, for example by making a suggestion. Find a balance between dismissing the other person's problem and taking on their problem as if it were your own.

Give yourself time to think

Do you get steam-rollered into doing things you do not want to do? Or take on extra commitments out of a sense of misplaced obligation? So often, when people ask us to do things, they also ask for an immediate response, and the sense of time pressure is catching. But few decisions really have to be made on the spot. A useful response is to say that you will think about it – and of course you also need to find out how long you have in which to think. The point of asking for time is that it helps you to keep things in perspective. It helps you to stand back from the immediate sense of pressure, to take stock, and to work out what you really want, especially when that is not immediately clear to you.

The skills involved in negotiation

Negotiation is only partly about trying to get something that you want. It is also about knowing how to do that fairly: without being aggressive, or manipulative; without moaning or whining or wheedling or demanding. Most people only start thinking about being in a negotiation at the point of confrontation. They leave it too late. Knowing how to negotiate means that you start off your interactions with other people, both at home and at work, without a warlike, aggressive or defensive attitude, thinking about how both of you can get what you want – to a degree. A counter-productive aspect of not knowing how to negotiate is the attitude that if you lose then someone else has won – or, conversely, if you are going to win, then you will have to get the better of someone else. This kind of attitude leads to confrontations, or to arguments, which most shy or socially anxious people go out of their way to avoid. Fear of provoking a confrontation or argument on the one hand, or of being steam-rollered on the other, makes it difficult to get what you want. Knowing how to negotiate makes it easier.

Developing a new perspective on negotiation, whether it is about who does what in the home or about differences of opinion or strategy at work, involves rethinking some of these assumptions about winning and losing. An alternative view, which has received much acclaim and which leads to much smoother relationships when two people want somewhat different things, is to think instead about the possibilities for mutual gain. Then no one has to be a loser, and when your wants and wishes are different from those of the people around you, there is no need to be dominated by the threat of personal loss (or defeat), or by the fear of your own or other people's aggression.

Box 12.1 lists some of the principles of cooperation. Negotiations are more likely to succeed, and to create ground for further negotiations later, if they are built upon these principles.

Handling difficult moments

There are, of course, endless ways in which our social lives can present us with difficulties, and three of these will be mentioned here. First, criticisms and complaints cause problems for socially anxious people because they so often fit with that person's self-opinion. If you expect to be judged negatively then receiving a criticism can easily confirm your opinion, and cast you down so far that it is hard to respond. Second, most people find confrontations and conflicts hard to deal with, particularly those worried about offending or alienating people, or who feel rejected and cast out when someone is angry with them. Finally, compliments, as well as being sometimes literally 'incredible', in the sense that they are just seem too far from reality to be believed, can make you feel so embarrassed that you want to shrink away. Personal remarks of many kinds tend to increase self-consciousness, and may provoke all the dreaded symptoms of social anxiety. Some of the ways of dealing with these three difficulties are described next.

BOX 12.1: SOME PRINCIPLES OF COOPERATION

- Think first about what the other person (or people) wants. What is their point of view? If you are not sure, then the first step is to find out. Ask rather than guess.
- Be open about what you want. This may feel risky, but it is one of the quickest ways to build up a sense of mutual trust.
- Do not sidestep the difficult issues. They clarify why negotiation is needed.
- Be prepared to give something up in order to get what you want most. This might open the way to constructive trading between you.
- Keep talking: not in the sense of monopolizing the air time, but in the sense of keeping the door open, so that communication goes on.
- However heated you feel, try not to resort to making personal comments, or slip into the opposite pattern of personalizing remarks that are made to you.
- When responding to someone else, make sure they know that you heard what they said first. Otherwise it is easy to react first and to think later.

Think in terms of building mutual trust.

Criticism and complaints

The key to dealing with complaints and criticisms is to be able to admit to weaknesses *accurately*, without either exaggerating their importance or dismissing them as irrelevant. Of course, when feelings run high this is not easy, and when the expression of those feelings has been stifled the underlying resentment and anger may make it even harder. The skills of cognitive therapy are helpful here. For example, if someone showed you they were pleased about something you had done, rather than displeased with you, and said: 'Thank you for being so helpful. That was really thoughtful of you,' would you generalize, and react as if this were a definitive judgment on your character? On the receiving end of a criticism ('That was really thoughtless. How could you be so insensitive?'), or when a complaint hits home and leaves you feeling rejected ('You're so messy – careless – forgetful – inefficient'), many people, and socially anxious ones in particular, treat the comment as if it were a profound statement of truth: as if it reflected a considered judgment about them, rather than a reaction to a particular thing they had done. But at times, everyone does things wrong, or insensitive things, or things that give offence or that others think are rude, and this no more makes them a villain than doing the opposite – being helpful or considerate or friendly – makes them a saint. The mistake is to judge the whole person, their whole character, on the basis of one, or a few, actions – whether for good or for bad.

When you are on the receiving end of criticisms and complaints it helps to refuse to be labelled, to accept what is true about the criticism and to apologize appropriately.

It is enormously helpful when doing this if you can be fair to yourself. Imagine what an impartial judge would say – not what the internal critic and socially anxious voice inside you wants to say. 'I'm sorry I upset you. I did not mean to' is often enough.

When you are in the opposite position, and yourself want to make a complaint or criticism, then there are three pointers to bear in mind.

1 *Be clear about what you want to say.* Say what you have to say briefly, without elaboration. This means sticking to the facts and not making guesses about the other person's feelings, or attitudes, or opinions. 'Your car was parked in front of my driveway again today.' 'I have been doing all the chores for both of us this week.'

2 *State your own feelings or opinions.* Be honest about what is bothering you without hot-headed displays of emotion: 'I needed to get my car out, and yours was in the way.' 'I feel taken for granted.'

3 *Specify what you want.* Ask for specific change. Ask for only one thing at a time. 'Please will you park somewhere else?' 'I would like some help clearing up, now.'

Obeying these 'rules', which may sound unrealistically simple at first sight, is useful because it takes people immediately out of conflict, during which feelings run high and are hard to control, and into negotiation, which is based on principles of fairness, instead.

Confrontation and conflict

When confrontation and conflict cannot be avoided it is important to know how to deal with them. When feelings are running high it is hard to think straight, and much easier to react first and to deal with the consequences – which often involve licking one's wounds – later. The following suggestions are not easy to follow, but will be useful if you can remember them. They are worth learning by heart, writing down in your notebook and practising. If they could only become second nature, much distress could be avoided. The main principles are these:

- Clarify what has upset you, and what is bothering the other person. Ask, and tell. 'I'm angry that you left me out.'
- Instead of assuming you are right and the other person is wrong, try to think in terms of different points of view. This helps even if one person *is* wrong.
- Watch out for escalation: in feelings, in threats, and in the way they are expressed. Often when people are angry on the surface, they are also fearful or hurt underneath, and paying attention to these feelings may solve the problem.

BOX 12.2: SOME RULES OF FAIR FIGHTING

- Keep to the point. Fight on one front at once, without bringing in ancient history.
- Cut out extremist words: 'You always ignore what I say.' 'You never pull your weight.'
- Take a break to calm down. Do not storm out, but explain what you are doing.
- Think about the part you play in the conflict, and own your own feelings: 'I'm angry about . . .', not 'You make me furious'.
- Do not hit where it hurts most. It makes it harder to forgive and forget.
- Blaming and threatening people leads to escalation, not to resolution.

Compliments

Compliments can create difficulties by causing embarrassment. Although you may blush with pleasure when complimented or admired, you may also blush with embarrassment, and wish that you could hide yourself away, as if you were facing a threat rather than a compliment. Why should a compliment make someone feel threatened? One reason is that it makes them the focus of attention, and attention has often been associated with threat in the past – even if this time the attention is positive rather than negative. Another is that responding to compliments involves using conventions, as if there were a 'formula' to apply. There sometimes seem to be a right way and a wrong way to respond to them. Being covered with confusion may happen partly because it is hard to think what to say.

Dismissing compliments is something for which socially anxious people may well have an overdeveloped skill: 'This old thing? I picked it up in a market years ago'; 'I only did what it said in the cookbook'; 'I had lots of help. It didn't have much to do with me, really'; and so on: anything to turn the attention elsewhere. They may fear being conceited or self-satisfied if they accept the compliment – reasoning that if you think too much of yourself, this could be another way in which other people could evaluate you negatively.

It is undoubtedly hard for some people to accept that the compliments they receive are genuine, and not just flattery, or motivated by wanting something from them. It is also hard to accept them gracefully. One way to learn is (genuinely) to give compliments to others, and to learn from their responses what to say yourself. Think about which ways feel right, and try them out. Do not dismiss compliments, or laugh them off, but try to accept them as one might accept another kind of appreciative offering. Ask yourself whether it would make a difference to believe in the compliment.

Striking a balance

If being assertive is about being fair, to yourself as well as to others, then it makes sense to sum up the main points made in this chapter by thinking about the numerous kinds of 'balancing acts' that are involved in overcoming social anxiety. Some of these are listed in Box 12.3, and you may like to add your own items to this list. The point is not to advise people to become fence-sitters, going for neither one thing nor the other, nor to make them into wishy-washy people with no strong opinions, but to help them to find a way of being themselves that involves neither controlling others nor being controlled by them – both of which are extremist positions. The danger of taking up extremist positions of these kinds it that one extreme seems to alternate with the other, making the business of finding the 'happy medium' even harder than usual. Extremist positions go with all-or-nothing thinking (either everything I do is useless, or it's all just fine), or with black-and-white thinking (If people don't love you, then they hate you), or with alternating between highs and lows (feeling wonderful about yourself when in a loving relationship, but desperately miserable, or incapable, or rejected when on your own).

BOX 12.3: BALANCING ACTS: ASSERTIVE BEHAVIOR AVOIDS EXTREMIST POSITIONS

- Being interested, but not too curious (or nosy).
- Focusing inwards, on your inner experience, as opposed to focusing outwards, only on other people.
- Talking versus listening.
- Seeking information on the one hand; disclosing information on the other.
- Talking only about feelings as against talking predominantly about facts.
- Recognizing the effects of the past on yourself without being dominated or restricted by it.

- Keeping yourself safe at one extreme, and barging in where angels fear to tread on the other.
- Revealing intimate things about yourself or clamming up, and saying nothing that might give you away, or give people a hold over you.
- Finding the half-way house between being passive and being aggressive.

13

The legacy of being bullied

Many socially anxious people have sad and horrible tales to tell about periods in their life when they were bullied, and still remember with acute distress what it felt like at the time. Being the subject of bullying can have long-lasting effects. Although there is no precise evidence that I know of to suggest that being bullied makes people socially anxious, and plenty of evidence to show that people of all sorts have been bullied at some time in their lives, regardless of whether they were shy or socially unconfident at the time, it is clear that some of the consequences of being bullied are especially difficult for socially anxious people to deal with. The purpose of this chapter is twofold: first to describe the longer-lasting effects of bullying that may have special relevance to shyness and social anxiety, and secondly to provide some ideas about how they can be overcome.

Some facts about bullying

Bullying is described in many books as 'primitive' behavior. What is meant by this is that it is often motivated by an almost instinctive desire to mask one's own vulnerability by controlling other people. If you are top dog, then you will be able to get your own way, and other people are less likely to attack you. This will be even more likely to work if you gather around you a group of followers (or henchmen).

Bullying can be found in all walks of life. It happens to adults as well as to children, at home, at school and at work, and it happens throughout the world. What is more, it is probably true to say that everyone has done it sometimes – to a degree. But mature people, supposedly, hardly ever do it; they do not need to, partly because they have learned how to negotiate, or to collaborate, or to live and to let live, and have no need to support themselves by gaining a hold over others.

Being fair – to yourself as well as to others – is the opposite of bullying. The skills of assertiveness, some of which were described in the last chapter, are some of the skills used by people for whom bullying is unnecessary and being bullied is irrelevant. But these skills alone may not be enough, especially when powerful social forces operate so as either to ignore or to condone bullying types of behavior. When it is hard, or even impossible, for one person to stand up against the group, then pressure to change has to be exerted on the culture or social context within which the bullying occurs.

Bullying can be both obvious and subtle, and it can range from relatively harmless and more or less affectionate kinds of teasing through to intimidation or victimization. Using threats and taunts are some of the most obvious bullying behaviors, and the more subtle ones may be harder to recognize at first. They include picking on people, or in some way singling them out for 'special' treatment; seeking out personal information and then disclosing it to others, or betraying a trust; excluding people, especially from positions of leadership, or isolating them; making general rather than specific criticisms and accusations that appear to apply to the whole person rather than to something that they did or said; sabotaging their plans or activities; making unreasonable demands; using gossip, innuendo or manipulation; and so on. Clearly, bullying is not just one thing: it involves many different kinds of language and behavior. What makes any of these bullying behavior is the intention to control or exclude people, so that they feel they no longer belong to the group to which the bully does belong. It works by making use of intimidation and humiliation.

Some effects of being bullied

Bullying exists in all degrees, from the relatively trivial to the horrendous. Being seriously bullied can be enormously stressful and affects every aspect of life: feelings or emotions, the body, all the levels of thinking that were described in Chapter 3, and behavior as well. For example, being bullied is frightening, but it can also make people feel angry, resentful, frustrated and, when it seems that there is nothing to be done about it and no way out, hopeless and depressed as well. It makes people physically tense, on edge, unable to relax or to sleep, and susceptible to visible symptoms of distress such as trembling or sweating. Their waking life may be dominated by a sense of dread, constantly keeping on the look out for 'dangerous' situations, by thoughts about what might happen next, and by memories or images of recent distressing experiences. Disturbing dreams may prevent them sleeping at night. Their daily behavior will be a product of all these experiences, which seriously interfere with their ability to do the things they wish to do, in the ways that they otherwise would.

However, the end result of being bullied varies greatly. For some people it appears to have no lasting effects, but for others it does more damage, and leaves an apparently permanent scar. Of course, the worse the bullying the worse the effects are likely to be, and the longer they are likely to last. But another factor is also important, and that is the meaning of the bullying to the person who was on the receiving end of it. The messages that different people take away with them at the time can play an important part in what happens next. For example, being tormented at school for being unable to pronounce your 'r's' properly could ultimately mean more about other people, and their ability to pick on irrelevancies when making judgments about you, than about you as a person, and it might then have no lasting effect on your self-opinion. On the other hand, it could leave you with a deep-seated uncertainty about yourself and your acceptability, and with your confidence shaken.

BOX 13.1: EFFECTS OF BULLYING, MAPPED ON TO FEATURES OF SOCIAL ANXIETY

Effects on beliefs, for example:
- I'm not acceptable as I am.
- I don't belong.
- People will reject me.
- Nobody can be trusted.

Effects on assumptions, for example:
- I've got to get people's approval, or they will exclude me.
- The only way not to be bullied is to hit before you get hit.
- If you let people get to know you they will take advantage of you.
- It's best not to tangle with powerful people, or with anyone in a position of authority.

Effects on attention, for example:
- Noticing people's frowns, or signs of criticism, or judgments.
- Checking out how you are coming over.

Effects on behaviors, including safety behaviours and avoidance, for example:
- Self-protective moves to hide your 'weaknesses'; secretiveness.
- Trying to please people, and to gain their approval; trying to do things 'right'.
- Keeping yourself to yourself; not joining in, or getting socially involved.
- Accommodating what you think others expect, for instance by hiding your anger.

Effects on self-consciousness and self-awareness, for example:
- Thinking about how you look, or speak, or behave.
- Making sure that you that you never say or do anything that might offend people.
- Embarrassment comes easily, for example when talking about personal feelings or needs.

The personal meaning to you of what happened helps to determine the precise form of the beliefs and assumptions that continue to influence you later on. It is in this way that the experience of bullying can link up with the features of social anxiety described earlier in this book, and some illustrations of the way in which this can happen are shown in Box 13.1.

The things that socially anxious people, and some shy people, tend to believe about themselves and about others clearly have something in common with the messages that being bullied can provide. Social anxiety focuses on the fear of being evaluated or judged: on the fear of doing something that will be humiliating or embarrassing; and bullies evaluate and judge their victims, and openly humiliate and embarrass them. It is hardly surprising that bullying can sometimes exacerbate social anxiety, and make it difficult to fight against it.

Reactions to being bullied

Many people blame themselves for being bullied, as if they have internalized the criticisms, accusations or taunts that they received and come to believe that they were true. Of course, there may have been an element of truth in them, as when children get picked on for their size or shape or colouring; or for some other characteristic for which they cannot be held responsible, but the truth does not justify the behavior. It is the bully and not the victim who is to blame, together with the system surrounding the bully that fails to prevent it happening. So, if you were bullied, that was not your fault.

Nor is it your fault if you could not find a way of stopping it. Many ways of responding to a bully have been found to make the problem worse, not better, at least on some occasions. If you tried them and failed, this does not mean that you were weak, or stupid, or not courageous enough. These include:

- explaining yourself, or justifying your behaviour
- seeking to gain approval, and to please the people who hurt you
- defending yourself or standing up for yourself
- giving as good as you got, or fighting back
- trying to let it ride over you; ignoring it and doing nothing about it

If people told you not to let it happen, or to show that you could give as good as you got, or if they left you with the impression that you asked for it, or laid yourself open to it, or deserved it in some way, then they too were wrong. Once again, the person who 'got it wrong' was the bully – not the target.

Understanding the bully

At this point, a word of understanding for children who bully does not come amiss. Bullies often feel extremely vulnerable themselves, and may not be well supported by the people around them. Their primitive need for acceptance and approval is often – though not necessarily – based on a potent sense of their own inadequacy or isolation. They may feel inferior and vulnerable too, and only have recourse to the more primitive ways of dealing with these feelings. They often pick on people who threaten them in some way, for example by being cleverer, or more competent, or more acceptable. This is why it is so important that schools develop clear policies for dealing with the problem, making it possible for both bullies and bullied to develop more mature ways of reacting to the challenges that confront them, and ensuring that they both receive more of the help and support that they need.

Overcoming the more enduring effects of being bullied

The main message here is: 'It's OK to be you.' As noted in Chapter 1, people who are shy and socially anxious have as many of the characteristics that people value and admire as everyone else, and there is no need to keep these characteristics hidden – from yourself or from others. Learning how to express them, and to develop them, helps to make you more spontaneous and less inhibited or self-conscious in your interactions with others, and this in turn develops the sense that you can trust yourself when with other people, and trust them not to attempt to manipulate or control you. All of the methods described in Part Two of this book can be used to help overcome the after-effects of being bullied, together with the skills described in Chapter 12 for making your voice heard in assertive ways. The following points are intended as reminders, and they are collected together here to help you to work out what to do if you feel that being bullied earlier in life has left you with a legacy that you would like now to leave behind.

Identify your internal critical voice

Do you have favourite ways of putting yourself down – 'I'm no good'; 'Imbecile'? A bad habit learned from bullies is to go to extremes when making judgments about yourself, and even to echo judgments that you have heard earlier. Try to remember what your bully said about you, and think again about the message it left you with. Try to free yourself from the old judgment and its painful implications by recognizing it for what it is: a primitive reaction made for primitive reasons that had nothing to do with your value or worth or acceptability *as a person* even then – let alone now. When you do something that bothers you, then it is the behavior that you should evaluate, and not yourself as a person. Watch out for any tendency to label yourself and take care not to overgeneralize, or you will be giving too much significance to one aspect of yourself or your behavior.

Identify your triggers

All sorts of things may remind you of some of the bad things that have happened to you earlier in life: actions of others; being spoken to in a certain tone of voice; a physical similarity with someone who bullied you; being around powerful or controlling people, or people who have authority over you; all sorts of sights, sounds, smells and so on.

Memories and images can be easily triggered, and they often bring strong feelings with them. They may also seem to come automatically, but are so fleeting that you may recognize a familiar feeling – of dread, or inferiority, or vulnerability of some kind – without being aware of what provoked it. For example, if you were cold-shouldered, excluded or ignored as a child, then similar feelings might be provoked in *any* situation in which you are not heard, such as when trying to catch the attention of a busy salesperson or the waiter in a restaurant.

Think about how your habitual reactions may maintain the problem

Imagine that you learned the hard way that it was dangerous to let people know too much about you. So you developed ways of not letting your reactions show, and keeping a deadpan expression on your face. At the time of being bullied this could well have been a sensible and effective reaction that averted some of the attacks that might otherwise have come your way. But this reserve can become a habit, and can easily be misinterpreted later on. It is surprising how many people with warm hearts and sensitive reactions, who develop ways of hiding their reactions in case they get picked on, come over as distant and cold when they feel nervous in company. These impressions may be so far from the truth that it is hard to acknowledge and to recognize them. It is as if they are built on an assumption that no longer holds: if I let people see my reactions I will be making myself a hostage to fortune. But they give the wrong impression to others. They mislead people about what you are really like. Although it can feel risky at first, showing your sensitivity and responsiveness helps people to warm to you, and to realize that the initial appearance of being cold or distant was wrong.

The general point here is that your original reactions to being bullied, while highly likely to have had adaptive, helpful aspects at the time, may subsequently keep the problem going. Think about how you originally reacted. Think about what you learned to do to protect yourself, or to keep yourself safe, and try to put these old reactions on hold for a while. See if doing so, when you have become more confident about taking the risk, makes a difference to your sense of being able to be yourself and to be at ease with that.

Re-examine your beliefs about your value or worth

Bullies often make people feel worthless: as if they had no value. If this is what you believe about yourself then your beliefs need updating. It is no wonder that this is the message that you took away at the time. It is hard not to believe the things that other people say about you when you are young and when these things are repeated and backed up by bullying tactics. The most important thing to remember is that your worth is never determined by what others think of you (good or bad), especially not if your evidence for such an undermining self-opinion comes from the opinion of someone who bullied you.

Develop a system of support

People who have been cast down by others need subsequently to be affirmed instead. In the end, it is being aware of one's own strengths and positive characteristics, one's talents and skills and preferences and interests, that provides a solid basis for self-affirmation. No one else can do it for you entirely, but having a network of supporters undoubtedly helps. Knowing that there are people who see your point of view reduces the sense of being alone and isolated. Letting them know how you think and feel about things, and being prepared to make your needs known, is one way of developing a sense of commonality: of shared ideas and attitudes, and even of shared experiences during childhood.

Concluding points

When overcoming the after-effects of bullying it helps, as in other contexts, to think in terms of striking a balance: a balance between pleasing other people and pleasing yourself; between seeking approval and ignoring what others think; between going your own way on your own and accommodating to what others want. In order to find out what suits you, and to develop the confidence to be yourself in the way that feels right, it would be useful to use mini-experiments, as described in Chapter 8, pp. 120–36. Then you can try things out and think carefully about what happens when you do. As mentioned at the beginning of this chapter, being yourself is fine. You just need to find out what makes you feel more confident and more comfortable about being the way that you are.

KEY POINTS

- Being bullied can have lasting effects, and these may be particularly hard for people who are socially anxious or shy to overcome.
- If you were bullied, that does not mean that it was your fault. Nor does it mean that you were too weak or inept to stop it happening. Bullying is 'primitive' behavior that is most effectively controlled by people leading the group in which it occurs.
- In order to get over the effects of having been bullied it is helpful to:
  - identify your critical voice;
  - identify the triggers that remind you of what happened;
  - think about how your reactions might work to maintain the problem;
  - re-examine your beliefs about your value and self-worth;
  - develop a system that provides you with support.
- Use some mini-experiments to help you to strike a balance between being controlled by others and protecting yourself by keeping yourself separate from them.

14

Relaxation

Anxiety and worry make you tense, and tension has a host of painful effects. It leads to physical aches and pains; it can make you tired and irritable; it can drag you down or wind you up; and it eats up energy fast. It is easy to recognize that it would help to be able to relax better, but it is not easy to do. There are now a great many books, videotapes and cassette tapes on relaxation available in the shops, and many health or leisure centres have information about local classes, so you may be able to find a method that you like quite easily. If not, the brief instructions on progressive muscular relaxation provided here provide a good starting point for teaching yourself how to relax.

Relaxation has to be learned

Life would be much easier if relaxation came naturally, but for many people it does not, and then it is necessary to make a conscious effort to learn how to do it. Relaxation is a skill, which means that if you are going to become good at it you will have to learn what to do and then practise doing it. One of the problems is that learning how to relax is not one thing, but many. It is:

- *an attitude*: taking things more in your stride, and more calmly
- *a physical skill*: learning how to recognize and release physical tension
- *a habit*: developing routines that wind you down rather than wind you up
- *restorative*: a way of giving yourself rest and recreation, that can be interesting, or stimulating, or pleasurable, as well as relaxing

There is plenty of research showing that people find relaxation helpful, but little comparing the different methods. Therefore it seems reasonable to choose whichever method attracts you and to stick with it. Whichever method you use, it is helpful to think of yourself as learning how to relax in four stages. First you need to prepare yourself, so that you can focus on what you are doing without being distracted; second, you need to practise relaxing, so that you know what you are trying to do; third, you need consciously to apply what you have learned, so that you can use it to help yourself; and fourth, you should think of extending what you have learned in ways that help you to adopt a relaxed lifestyle. Going through these four stages will help you to take advantage of all the different aspects of relaxation, and one way of doing it, using progressive muscular relaxation, is described below.

Stage 1: Preparation

Find yourself time, and find yourself a comfortable place in which to practise. You will need at least half an hour a day at first, and if you are a busy person – or a disorganized one – it may be hard to set yourself a regular routine and to stick to it. You should make sure that you will not be disturbed while you are practising (even unplugging the telephone before you begin), and your comfortable place needs to support your body well, and to be warm. Many of the relaxation methods can be learned either sitting or lying down, but if you do them in bed, late at night, you may find that you fall asleep while you are doing them. Although you may want to use the method later on to help you to sleep better, it is more sensible at first to practise relaxing when you are not likely to fall asleep so that you can concentrate on the things you are supposed to be learning: how to recognize the many differences between being tense and being relaxed, how to pick up your own signs of tension and trouble spots, and – most important of all – how to let them go when you feel you need to.

Having made yourself comfortable, start by focusing on your breathing, and trying to breathe in a relaxed and calm way. Relaxed breathing is slow and regular, and when you are deeply relaxed your stomach will rise and fall as you breathe in and out. Tense breathing is relatively rapid and shallow, and it makes your chest move up and down, sometimes quite rapidly. One way to learn about your breathing is to place one hand on your chest and one on your stomach and to see which moves most. If you do this at a time when you are really relaxed you will find that the hand on your chest hardly moves at all. If you are breathing in a tense way then just try to slow yourself down gently, by degrees. You could pace yourself by counting slowly as you breathe out, saying, for example, 'one thousand, two thousand, three thousand . . .' Try to ensure that you have completely emptied your lungs before you inhale again. It may also help to say something to yourself, like 'let go', as you breathe out, to start yourself thinking about being more relaxed.

When you are learning to relax, go at your own pace. There is no hurry, and becoming impatient or self-conscious about it can be counter-productive.

Stage 2: Practice

Learn to relax your body by first tensing up and then letting go groups of muscles, one by one. This works well because it is hard, when you are tense, to obey the instruction 'relax', but it is relatively easy to focus on one part of your body at a time and to tighten up those muscles even if they are already somewhat tense. Doing so, for example by clenching your fists, makes you immediately aware of the tension in those muscles. When they start to ache or to hurt then it is easy to let them go, and tensing up first helps them to relax more fully than they otherwise might. When you relax after tensing your muscles up you may even feel the blood flow back again, making you feel warmer as you become more deeply relaxed. If you breathe out as you let the muscles go you will be using the body's natural rhythms to help you to relax.

The basic exercise is simple. Tense up a particular group of muscles. Hold the tension for a short while. Then let the tension go. If you can breathe out when you let go, you will find that it helps in letting the tension subside even further. Give yourself time for all the tension to drain away before you move on to tighten up the next part of your body. You could tell yourself to relax, or to let go, as you exhale for the next few breaths, so that you make a conscious association between giving yourself this message and the feeling of being more relaxed. You could also imagine your body becoming increasingly heavy, or limp, or floppy as the tension in it dies away.

Focus on each part of your body in turn, repeating the same basic exercise. As you progress, try to concentrate fully on each part of the body, and to tense the next bit up without losing too much of the relaxation that you have already achieved. Usually people learn to relax their hands and arms first, then work up from their feet to their head, in the order shown in Box 14.1.

Do not leap up quickly after doing your relaxation exercises, or you might feel dizzy; give yourself time to start up gradually.

Stage 3: Application

No one can remain deeply relaxed while carrying out normal daily activities, nor while feeling anxious or worried, so the next step is to learn how to apply what you have learned in ways that will be more useful. If you can recognize small degrees of tension early, before they have built up, it will be easier to relax your way out of them. To do this you need to shorten the exercises and to practise relaxing in increasingly difficult situations.

BOX 14.1: PROGRESSIVE MUSCULAR RELAXATION

Working through the parts of the body in a regular order helps you not to forget any of the muscle groups. Focus your attention on each part of the body as you tense it up, then give yourself as much time as you need to let all the tension go. As you learn how to relax you may notice small degrees of tension more easily. If you find it difficult to release tension in one place, such as your neck, or back, you may need a double dose of the basic exercise for that part of your body.

Hands: Clench the fists. Hold the tension for a while before you let go.

Arms: Tighten up your biceps and lower arms, e.g. by pushing them down.

Shoulders: Raise your shoulders as if they could touch your ears.

Feet: Screw up your toes.

Front of legs: Point your toes as you stretch your leg out.

Back of legs: Flex your feet up and push your heels away from you.

Thighs: Tighten them as you press your knees down.

Bottom: Clench your buttocks together.

Stomach: Hold your stomach muscles in tight.

Lower back: Press the small of your back into the chair or floor.

Chest: Breathe in, hold your breath, and tighten your chest muscles.

Shoulders: Raise your shoulders to touch your ears. Breathe in as you tighten up.

Neck: (1) Stretch your head up, as if your chin could touch the ceiling.

(2) Bend your head forward until your chin reaches your chest.

Mouth and jaw: Press your lips together and clench your teeth.

Eyes: Close them up tight.

Forehead and scalp: Raise your eyebrows as if they could disappear into your hair.

Face: Screw all the muscles up together.

There are many ways of shortening relaxation exercises, for example working on the body in bigger chunks (arms, legs, body and face); working through the first few exercises and then focusing on the other parts of your body to see if you can become aware of the remaining tension and let it go; or leaving out the tension and working only on the relaxation. Shortened exercises are usually more helpful if they include an instruction to yourself, like 'keep calm', and you start by trying to breathe in a relaxed way. The more practice you give yourself, the quicker this stage will go. So once you can relax more quickly in peace and quiet, start trying to apply the method in other situations also. Remind yourself often as you go through the day to check your level of tension. Then you could take a deep breath in, hold it for a moment and as you let it go drop your shoulders and tell yourself to relax. Or you could set your watch to bleep every so often and do one small tense and relax exercise every time you hear it. The shorter your exercise, the more often you should practise.

If you find it easier to relax physically than mentally, then you may also find it useful consciously to bring relaxing images into your mind as you practise relaxing. The images you choose should be those that have strong associations for you with being relaxed. The sorts of things that other people choose include being in a quiet, peaceful part of the country; looking into a picture of something beautiful, watching the sea or the sky when the weather is calm, or being somewhere warm and comfortable where – at least temporarily – no demands will be made upon you. Try consciously to turn your mind, when it wanders to your fears or worries, to one of these images instead, and make use of all your senses in the imagery, so that you might become aware of what you could hear, feel and smell in your image, as well as what you could see.

Do not be surprised if your images change, and your mind wanders away from them, as images constantly change. However, if your mind wanders back to the things that make you feel tense then try to re-establish the more relaxing imagery, and start again from there.

It is always easier to relax when you can start by making yourself comfortable in a quiet and warm place. Once you are reasonably sure that you know how to do it, try doing brief relaxation exercises when you are sitting at a table, or walking somewhere, or eating a meal. Practise relaxing while carrying out everyday activities first, and then move on to relaxing when doing something more difficult for you, like talking on the telephone. You will certainly not be able to apply your relaxation skills in situations that make you extremely anxious at first, but the more practice you have the more you will improve – and you can certainly use them to help you calm down after being in a tight spot. Develop your skills by applying them as often as you can, especially if you are taken by surprise by a situation that troubles you.

Stage 4: Extension

Being relaxed is an attitude as well as the result of learning a practical skill. Here are some ways to develop a more relaxed attitude.

- *Adopt a relaxed posture.* Do you find yourself sitting on the edge of your chair? Or fidgeting and fiddling with things? Or hurrying about with your head tucked into your shoulders and your eyes on the ground? Tension wastes energy, so allow your body to rest whenever you can.
- *Stop rushing about.* This is an exhausting habit, and quickly wears you out. Most people get just as much done when they do it more slowly and calmly, and they can also keep going for longer, at a more relaxed pace.
- *Plan to do some things that you find relaxing.* It does not matter whether these things are strenuous (like gardening, or going for a run), or more peaceful (like listening to music or watching TV). It is the fact that they help you to relax that is helpful.
- *Seek out things that you enjoy, and that give you pleasure.* The more you are enjoying yourself, the more relaxed you will feel.
- *Spread the risks.* If you put all your eggs in one basket, a threat to that basket will make you extremely tense.
- *Give yourself breaks.* Take short breaks, like half an hour looking at a magazine, as well as longer ones, like a day out or a holiday.

Useful Information

Useful organizations and online services

Great Britain

British Association of Behavioural and Cognitive Psychotherapies (BABCP)
The Globe Centre
PO Box 9
Accrington BB5 0XB
Tel: 01254 875 277
Email: babcp@babcp.com
Website: www.babcp.org.uk

British Association for Counselling and Psychotherapy (BACP)
BACP House
15 St John's Business Park
Lutterworth
Leicestershire LE17 4HB
Tel: 0870 443 5252
Email: bacp@bacp.co.uk
Website: www.bacp.co.uk

FearFighter
Website: www.fearfighter.com

(This website helps sufferers to identify specific problems and develop and work on treatment of those problems)

MIND: The National Association for Mental Health
Granta House
15–19 Broadway
Stratford
London E15 4BQ
MindinfoLine: 0845 766 0163
Email: contact@mind.org.uk

No Panic
93 Brands Farm
Randlay
Telford TF3 2JQ
Helpline: 0808 808 0545 (10 a.m. – 10 p.m.)
Email: ceo@nopanic.org.uk
Website: www.nopanic.org.uk

Social Anxiety UK
Email: contact@social-anxiety.org.uk
Website: www.social-anxiety.org.uk

Australia

**Anxiety Disorders
Association, Victoria
(ADAVIC)**
PO Box 625
Kew
VIC 3101
Tel: 0061 03 9853 8089
Email: adavic@adavic.org.au
Website:
home.vicnet.net.au/~adavic/

**Social Anxiety Australia
(SAA)**
PO Box 94
Indooroopilly
Queensland
Australia 4068
Tel: 0061 07 3366 7726
Email:
contact@socialanxiety.com.au
Website: www.socialanxiety
australia.com.au

New Zealand

**Social Anxiety Support
Group**
Floor 2
Securities House
221 Gloucester Street
PO Box 13167
Christchurch
Tel: 0064 03 377 9665

Fax: 0064 03 365 5345
Website:
www.socialphobia.org.nz

USA

**Anxiety Disorders
Association of America
(ADAA)**
Tel: 001 240 485 1001
Fax: 001 240 485 1035
Website: www.adaa.org

**The Association for
Behavioral and Cognitive
Therapies (ABCT)
(Formerly the Association
for the Advancement of
Behavior Therapy)**
305 7th Avenue
16th Floor
New York NY 10001
Tel: 001 212 647 1890
Fax: 001 212 647 1865
Website: www.aabt.org

**Institute for Behavior
Therapy**
104 East 40th Street
Suite 206
New York NY 10016
Tel: 001 212 692 9288
Fax: 001 212 692 9305

Social Phobia/Social Anxiety
Association (SP/SAA)
2058 E. Topeka Drive
Phoenix AZ 85024
Website:
www.socialphobia.org

Social Anxiety Institute
(SAI)
Website: www.socialanxiety
institute.org

Useful books

Edmund J. Bourne, *The Anxiety and Phobia Workbook* (fourth
edition), Oakland, New Harbinger Publications 2005

Martha Davis, Elizabeth Robbins Eshelman and Matthew
McKay, *The Relaxation and Stress Reduction Workbook* (fifth
edition), Oakland, New Harbinger Publications, 2000

Melanie Fennell, *Overcoming Low Self-esteem*, London,
Robinson, 1999

Dennis Greenberger and Christine Padesky, *Mind over Mood*,
New York, Guilford Press, 1995

Debra Hope, Richard G. Heimberg and Cynthia L. Turk,
Managing Social Anxiety, New York, Oxford University
Press Inc., 2006

Helen Kennerley, *Overcoming Anxiety*, London, Robinson, 1997

Harriet G. Lerner, *The Dance of Anger*, New York,
HarperCollins, 1999

Matthew McKay, Carole Honeychurch and Patrick Fanning,
The Self-esteem Companion, Oakland, New Harbinger
Publications, 2005

Thich Nhat Hanh, *The Miracle of Mindfulness*, London, Rider,
1991

Ronald M. Rapee, *Overcoming Shyness and Social Phobia*, New
York, Jason Aronson, 1998

Sue Spence, Ronald M. Rapee and Vanessa Cobham, *Helping
Your Anxious Child*, Oakland, New Harbinger Publications,
2000

Appendix

In this appendix you will find blank copies of the various worksheets described in the earlier chapters. These are for you to copy if you wish, so that you can use them to continue the work on overcoming your social anxiety. One study has shown that people working on their own who do not complete any written work improve less than people who do. So if you complete some of these worksheets while working at overcoming your problem you will be more likely to make the gains that you want to make. It is useful to copy these blank worksheets, and also to keep some spares in a safe place, so that you will be able to pick one up if you unexpectedly have good reason to need it.

There are many different versions of worksheets to help people change, in many different books. So if the particular version provided does not suit you, there is no reason why you should not make one up to suit your needs better. Check that you have understood what it is intended for first, and then make whatever adaptations seem sensible to you.

TABLE 7.1: THOUGHT RECORD FOR IDENTIFYING THOUGHTS

(for completed examples see pages 137)

Situation (be specific)	Feelings (there may be more than one)	Thoughts, impressions, etc. (keep the different thoughts separate)

Key questions for step 1: Identifying your thoughts

- What went through your mind when you started to feel anxious? And after that? And when it was all over?

- What was the worst thing that might have happened at the time?

- What is it about this situation that matters to you?

- What does having this experience mean to you?

- What does it mean about you?

TABLE 7.1: THOUGHT RECORD FOR IDENTIFYING THOUGHTS

(for completed examples see pages 137)

Situation (be specific)	Feelings (there may be more than one)	Thoughts, impressions, etc. (keep the different thoughts separate)

TABLE 7.1: THOUGHT RECORD FOR IDENTIFYING THOUGHTS

(for completed examples see pages 137)

Situation (be specific)	Feelings (there may be more than one)	Thoughts, impressions, etc. (keep the different thoughts separate)

TABLE 7.2: THOUGHT RECORD FOR LOOKING FOR ALTERNATIVES

(for completed examples see pages 146)

Upsetting thoughts (take one at a time)	Possible alternatives (there may be more than one)

Key questions for step 2: Looking for alternatives

- *What are the facts?* What evidence do you have to support what you think? What evidence is there against it? Which way of thinking fits best with the facts? The fact that you think something does not make it true.

- *What possible alternatives are there?* What would you think if you were more confident? How might someone else view this situation? What would you say to someone else who was thinking in this sort of way? What would someone who cared about you say?

- *What is the worst possible way of seeing things,* or the worst thing that could possibly happen? What is the best way of seeing things, or the best thing that could happen? Which is most realistic? Or most likely to be right?

- *What biases might be affecting your thinking?* For example, are you jumping to conclusions? Exaggerating? Over-generalizing? Are you predicting the future as a certainty? Or mindreading? Or focusing on the negative side of things at the expense of everything else?

- *What can you do that would be helpful?* What personal skills and strengths do you have to help? What past experience of dealing with similar problems? What help, advice and support are available to you, from others or from books? What can you do to change things? If you can't change the situation, can you keep an open mind about what it means?

TABLE 7.2: THOUGHT RECORD FOR LOOKING FOR ALTERNATIVES

(for completed examples see pages 146)

Upsetting thoughts (take one at a time)	Possible alternatives (there may be more than one)

TABLE 7.2: THOUGHT RECORD FOR LOOKING FOR ALTERNATIVES

(for completed examples see pages 146)

Upsetting thoughts (take one at a time)	Possible alternatives (there may be more than one)

TABLE 7.3: COMPLETE THOUGHT RECORD

(for completed examples see pages 155)

Situation (be specific)	Upsetting thoughts (keep the different thoughts separate)	Possible alternatives (there may be more than one)	Change in feelings (–10–0–+10)	Action plan (what would you like to do differently?)

TABLE 7.3: COMPLETE THOUGHT RECORD

(for completed examples see pages 155)

Situation (be specific)	Upsetting thoughts (keep the different thoughts separate)	Possible alternatives (there may be more than one)	Change in feelings (−10–0–+10)	Action plan (what would you like to do differently?)

TABLE 8.2: THOUGHT RECORD FOR CHANGING BEHAVIORS

(for completed examples see pages 176)

Specific situation [Think of a situation in which you use a safety behavior]	Prediction [What will happen if you do not keep yourself safe? How will you know if it happens?]	Experiment [How will you find out? What will you do differently?]	What actually happened? [What did you observe? Stick to the facts.]	Conclusions [What does this mean?]

TABLE 8.2: THOUGHT RECORD FOR CHANGING BEHAVIORS

(for completed examples see pages 176)

Specific situation [Think of a situation in which you use a safety behavior]	Prediction [What will happen if you do not keep yourself safe? How will you know if it happens?]	Experiment [How will you find out? What will you do differently?]	What actually happened? [What did you observe? Stick to the facts.]	Conclusions [What does this mean?]

Key questions for changing beliefs

- Would you judge someone else who felt like you do in the same way? What would you say to someone else who held a belief like this one?

- Are you being fair to yourself?

- Are you going in for 'character assassination', rather than sticking to what happened on one particular occasion?

- Are you forgetting that everyone makes mistakes, gets things wrong, and feels socially uncomfortable at times? That no one can be perfect?

- Are you ignoring your strengths and focusing on your weaknesses? Ignoring the successes and friendships, while focusing on failures and embarrassments?

- Are you falling into a biased pattern of thinking? Catastrophizing? Taking things personally? Mind reading? Emotional reasoning? (See the list on page 140.)

- Are you drawing conclusions on the basis of your childhood or adolescent experiences?

- Are you judging yourself as you have (once) been judged? If so, what makes the person, or people, who judged you right now? Who is the best authority on you? Other people or yourself?

BOX 10.2: COUNTER-BELIEF WORKSHEET

(for completed examples see pages 239–40)

Belief:

How much do you believe this (0–100 per cent)?

The Forward Search Plan

BEFORE THE EVENT
1 Think of a future situation that will be difficult for you

2 Your expectation or prediction (this should fit with your belief)

3 Search plan: What should you be looking out for?

AFTER THE EVENT
4 Outcome: What actually happened?

5 What conclusions can you draw from that?

Rethinking your original belief
How much do you believe it now (0–100 per cent)?

Does your belief need modifying? If so, how?

BOX 10.2: COUNTER-BELIEF WORKSHEET

(for completed examples see pages 239–40)

Belief:

How much do you believe this (0–100 per cent)?

The Forward Search Plan

BEFORE THE EVENT
1 Think of a future situation that will be difficult for you

2 Your expectation or prediction (this should fit with your belief)

3 Search plan: What should you be looking out for?

AFTER THE EVENT
4 Outcome: What actually happened?

5 What conclusions can you draw from that?

Rethinking your original belief
How much do you believe it now (0–100 per cent)?

Does your belief need modifying? If so, how?

BOX 10.2: COUNTER-BELIEF WORKSHEET

(for completed examples see pages 239–40)

Belief:

How much do you believe this (0–100 per cent)?

The Forward Search Plan

BEFORE THE EVENT
1 Think of a future situation that will be difficult for you

2 Your expectation or prediction (this should fit with your belief)

3 Search plan: What should you be looking out for?

AFTER THE EVENT
4 Outcome: What actually happened?

5 What conclusions can you draw from that?

Rethinking your original belief
How much do you believe it now (0–100 per cent)?

Does your belief need modifying? If so, how?

Index

Numbers in bold indicate primary reference

GILLIAN BUTLER is a Fellow of the British Psychological Society and a founder member of the Academy of Cognitive Therapy. She works both for the NHS and for Oxford Cognitive Therapy Centre. Through ten years of clinical research with the University of Oxford, she helped to develop and evaluate cognitive behavioral treatments for social phobia and for Generalized Anxiety Disorder. She has a special clinical interest in the use of CBT during recovery from traumatic experiences in childhood and runs training workshops on a wide variety of topics relevant to practitioners of CBT, in the UK and other countries. She is particularly interested in making the products of research available to the general public and, in addition to being the author of *Overcoming Social Anxiety and Shyness*, she is co-author of *Manage Your Mind: The Mental Fitness Guide* and of *Psychology: A Very Short Introduction*.

The aim of the **Overcoming** series is to enable people with a range of
common problems and disorders to take control of their own recovery program.
Each title, with its specially tailored program, is devised by a practising
clinician using the latest techniques of cognitive behavioral therapy –
techniques which have been shown to be highly effective in changing the
way patients think about themselves and their problems.
The series was initiated in 1993 by Peter Cooper, Professor of Psychology
at Reading University and Research Fellow at the University of Cambridge
in the UK whose original volume on overcoming bulimia nervosa and binge-eating continues
to help many people in the USA, the UK and Europe. Many books in the Overcoming series
are recommended by the UK Department of Health under the Books on Prescription scheme.

Other titles in the series include:

All titles in the series are available by mail order.
Please see the order form at the back of this book.
www.overcoming.co.uk